Athanasius, whose name means 'immortal,' lives on in this comprehensive and commendable biography. Barnes shows how the animated controversialist managed a full life, as a Nicene theologian, Alexandrian bishop, and five-time refugee. The influence of the patriarch persists through these informed pages.

Paul A. Hartog
Professor of Theology, Faith Baptist Theological Seminary, Ankeny, Iowa

EARLY CHURCH FATHERS
SERIES EDITORS
MICHAEL A. G. HAYKIN & SHAWN WILIHITE

ATHANASIUS
OF HIS LIFE & IMPACT
ALEXANDRIA

PETER BARNES

CHRISTIAN
FOCUS

Peter Barnes is an Australian Presbyterian pastor who worked in Vanuatu, then Nambucca River on the mid-north coast of New South Wales, and now in Revesby in Sydney. With a doctorate on the impact of biblical criticism on the NSW Presbyterian Church from 1865-1915, he has taught Church History on a part-time basis for over thirty years at Christ College in Burwood NSW. He is married to Lyn, and they have six grown children, and a growing number of grandchildren.

Copyright © Peter Barnes 2019

Peter Barnes has asserted his right under the Copyright, Designs and Patents Act, 1988, to be identified as Author of this work.

paperback ISBN 978-1-5271-0392-4
epub ISBN 978-1-78191-0453-2
Mobi ISBN 978-1-78191- 0454-9

First published in 2019
by
Christian Focus Publications Ltd,
Geanies House, Fearn, Ross-shire
IV20 1TW, Scotland

www.christianfocus.com

A CIP catalogue record for this book is available from the British Library.

Cover designed by MOOSE77
Printed by Bell & Bain, Glasgow

CONTENTS

Series preface..9

A Chronology of Athanasius of Alexandra............................ 13

Foreword 17

1. 'The Divine Power has raised you up to be as *Contra Mundum*': *Life in Alexandria during the Diocletian Persecution and the Rise of Constantine* 21

2. 'His Word and His Wisdom must be Everlasting': *Development of Early Christology and the Way to Nicaea* 39

3. 'We Believe in One God ...': *The Council of Nicaea and its Immediate Aftermath* 57

4. 'Begotten of the Father without Beginning and Eternally': *A Continued Post-Nicene Christological Conflict between Athanasius and the Empire*...................................... 69

5. 'For His Mercy Endures Forever': *Athanasian Exiles, the Beginning of the Demise of Arianism, and the Final Years of Athanasius's Life*................................. 85

6. 'For He Became Man ...': *A Summary of Athanasius's Theology and Introduction to* On the Incarnation *and* Against the Gentiles................... 123

7. 'A Man in Christ': *Athanasius's View of the Bible, Asceticism and Spirituality*... 147

8. 'Christ loved us in His great love and ascended a cross for our sake': *The Influence and Estimation of Athanasius's Life* 159

Brief Glossary..167

DEDICATION

To Lyn for all she is and does.

SERIES PREFACE

On reading the Church Fathers

By common definition, the Church Fathers are those early Christian authors who wrote between the close of the first century, right after the death of the last of the apostles, namely the apostle John, and the middle of the eighth century. In other words, they were those figures who were active in the life of the church between the time of Ignatius of Antioch and Clement of Rome (who penned writings at the very beginning of the second century), and the Venerable Bede and John of Damascus (who stood at the close of antiquity and the onset of the Middle Ages). Far too many Evangelicals in the modern day know next to nothing about these figures. Series editor Michael Haykin will never forget being asked to give a mini-history conference at a church in southern Ontario. He suggested three talks on three figures from Latin-speaking North Africa: Perpetua, Cyprian, and Augustine. The leadership of the church came back to him seeking a different set of names, since they had never heard of the first two figures, and while they had heard of the third name, the famous bishop of Hippo Regius, they really knew nothing about him. He gave them another list of post-Reformation figures for the mini-conference, but privately thought that not knowing anything about these figures was possibly a very good reason to have a conference on them! He suspected that such ignorance is quite widespread among those who call themselves Evangelicals—hence the importance of this small series of studies on a select number of Church Fathers, to educate and inform God's people about their forebears in the faith.

Past appreciation for the Fathers
How different is the modern situation from the past, when many of our Evangelical and Reformed forebears knew and treasured the writings of the ancient church. The French Reformer John Calvin, for example, was ever a keen student of the Church Fathers. He did not always agree with them, even when it came to one of his favorite authors, namely, Augustine. But Calvin was deeply aware of the value of knowing their thought and drawing upon the riches of their written works for elucidating the Christian Faith in his own day. And in the seventeenth century, the Puritan theologian John Owen, rightly called the 'Calvin of England' by some of his contemporaries, was not slow to turn to the experience of the one he called 'holy Austin', namely Augustine, to provide him with a pattern of God the Holy Spirit's work in conversion.

Yet again, the Particular Baptist John Gill turned to the Fathers to help him elucidate the biblical teaching regarding the blessed Trinity when he was faced with the anti-Trinitarianism of the Deist movement in the early eighteenth century, and other Protestant bodies (for instance, the English Presbyterians, the General Baptists, and large tracts of Anglicanism) who were unable to retain a firm grasp on this utterly vital biblical doctrine. Gill's example in this regard influenced other Baptists like John Sutcliff, pastor of the Baptist cause in Olney, where John Newton also ministered. Sutcliff was so impressed by the *Letter to Diognetus*, which he wrongly supposed to have been written by Justin Martyr, that he translated it for *The Biblical Magazine*, a Calvinistic publication with a small circulation. He sent it to the editor of this periodical with the commendation that this second-century work is 'one of the most valuable pieces of ecclesiastical antiquity'.

One final caveat

One final word about the Fathers recommended in this small series of essays. The Fathers are not Scripture. They are senior conversation partners about Scripture and its meaning. We listen to them respectfully, but are not afraid to disagree when they err. As the Reformers rightly argued, the writings of the Fathers must be subject to Scripture. John Jewel, the Anglican apologist, put it well when he stated in 1562:

'But what say we of the fathers, Augustine, Ambrose, Jerome, Cyprian, etc.? What shall we think of them, or what account may we make of them? They be interpreters of the word of God. They were learned men, and learned fathers; the instruments of the mercy of God, and vessels full of grace. We despise them not, we read them, we reverence them, and give thanks unto God for them. They were witnesses unto the truth, they were worthy pillars and ornaments in the church of God. Yet may they not be compared with the word of God. We may not build upon them: we may not make them the foundation and warrant of our conscience: we may not put our trust in them. Our trust is in the name of the Lord.'

Series Editors:
Michael A. G. Haykin
Chair and Professor of Church History
The Southern Baptist Theological Seminary,
Louisville, Kentucky and

Shawn J. Wilhite
Professor of Christian Studies
California Baptist University,
Riverside, California

A CHRONOLOGY OF ATHANASIUS
OF ALEXANDRIA

A.D. 298/299   Athanasius born

303   Persecution under Diocletian begins

306   Constantine becomes emperor

312   Constantine victorious at the Battle
                  of the Milvian Bridge outside Rome

318   Arian controversy breaks out

324   Constantine becomes sole emperor

325   Council of Nicaea, where Athanasius
                  attends as deacon and assistant to
                  Bishop Alexander of Alexandria

328	Athanasius becomes bishop of Alexandria
335	Council of Tyre condemns Athanasius
335-337	Athanasius's first exile in Augusta Treverorum in Gaul (today Trier, Germany); possible date for his writing of On the Incarnation of the Word
337	Constantine dies
339-346	Athanasius's second exile, in Rome, under Constantius II
341	Athanasius condemned at the Dedication Council of Antioch
343	Athanasius defended by the western council at Serdica, but condemned by the eastern council
356-362	Athanasius's third exile, in the desert, by order of Constantius II; writes Life of Antony and The Letters to Serapion on the Holy Spirit
362	Council of Alexandria

362-363   Athanasius's fourth exile, by order of Julian

365-366   Athanasius's fifth exile

373   Death of Athanasius

381   Council of Constantinople

FOREWORD

'Those who do away with Christian doctrine are, whether they are aware of it or not, the worst enemies of Christian living ... The coals of orthodoxy are necessary to the fire of piety.'[1] How often have these words of the Victorian Baptist preacher Charles Haddon Spurgeon, uttered at the height of what is called the Down-grade controversy, been proven true in the history of the church. And nowhere more so than in *the* great controversy that wracked the Christian world during the fourth century, namely the Arian controversy. This struggle over the nature of the Godhead, which ran from the late A.D. 310s to the early 380s, engaged the talents of some of the most gifted theologians of the ancient church, men such as Hilary of Poitiers (c.315-367/368), Ambrose of Milan (c.339-397) and the Cappadocian Fathers—Basil of Caesarea (c.330-379), his brother Gregory of Nyssa (c.335-c.395), and their mutual friend Gregory of Nazianzus (c.329-389/390) and above all, Athanasius (c.299-373). In fact, Athanasius has been rightly described by historian Ivor J.

---

1.   Charles Haddon Spurgeon, 'How can you have the Shadow without the Tree?', *The Sword and the Trowel* (1887), p. 62. For help in locating this quote I am indebted to Mr Ian Clary, my research assistant.

Davidson as 'one of the most significant figures in Christian history'.[2]

Athanasius's significance does not lie in his having constructed an influential systematic theology like the sixteenth-century Reformer John Calvin, nor in his being a theologian whose work covered a vast multiplicity of subjects, like that of Augustine (354-430). Rather, as the Athanasian scholar Archibald Robertson (1853-1931) pointed out, Athanasius's 'theological greatness lies in his firm grasp of soteriological principles, in his resolute subordination of everything else ... to the central fact of Redemption, and to what that fact implied as to the Person of the Redeemer'.[3] This soteriological focus in turn stemmed from a single-minded love for Christ and, in Robertson's words, an absorption with the 'glory of God and the welfare of the Church'.[4] Until his death in 373, Athanasius was the most formidable opponent of Arianism in the Roman Empire. Ultimately, for him, this fight was not a struggle for ecclesial power[5] or even for the rightness of his theological position. It was a battle for the souls of men and women. Athanasius rightly knew that upon one's view of Christ hung one's eternal destiny. As he wrote to the bishops of Egypt in 356: 'as therefore the struggle that is now set before us concerns *all that we are*, either to reject or to keep the faith, let us be zealous and resolve to guard what we have received, bearing in

---

2.   A Public Faith: From Constantine to the Medieval World, A.D. 312–600 (The Baker History of the Church, vol.2; Grand Rapids, MI: Baker Books, 2005), p. 39.

3.   Archibald Robertson, 'Prolegomena' to Select Writings and Letters of Athanasius, Bishop of Alexandria (Nicene and Post-Nicene Fathers, Second Series, vol.4; repr. Grand Rapids: Wm. B. Eerdmans Publ. Co., 1971), p. lxix.

4.   Ibid., p. lxvii.

5.   Pace the view of many twentieth- and twenty-first-century scholars of this period. See the extremely helpful study of Duane Wade-Hampton Arnold, The Early Episcopal Career of Athanasius of Alexandria (Notre Dame/London: University of Notre Dame Press, 1991), especially pages 175-186. Arnold quotes Adolf von Harnack's 'slightly overstated' estimate of Athanasius: 'If we measure him by the standards of his time, we can discover nothing ignoble or weak about him' (Early Episcopal Career of Athanasius, p. 186).

mind the confession that was written down at Nicaea'.[6] And by God's grace, his victory in that struggle has been of enormous blessing to the church ever since.

From Peter Barnes's superb study of Athanasius's life and thought that follows, three lessons impressed themselves upon this reader. First, utterly critical to the Christian faith is the full deity of Christ and His Holy Spirit. If they are not both fully God, as much God as God the Father is God, then our gospel is a sham. If the Son and the Spirit are not both fully divine, then our salvation is bereft of reality. To quote Athanasius, 'Jesus'—and one can add *and the Holy Spirit*—'whom I know as my redeemer cannot be less than God.' Second, Athanasius knew beyond a shadow of a doubt that a genuinely Christian theology is a Trinitarian theology. He would have agreed with one of his early admirers, Gregory of Nazianzus, when the latter said: 'when I say God, I mean Father, Son and Holy Spirit'.[7] Third, and final, we can learn from his dogged determination to be faithful to his divine Lord—summed up by the slogan *Athanasius contra mundum* ('Athanasius against the world'). He refused to give way to political pressure and physical force from a succession of Arian emperors, for he rightly believed the faith of Nicaea to be that of the Scriptures. Athanasius knew that there were such essential doctrines in the Scriptures that to lose them was to lose biblical Christianity. And so a true Christian must be prepared to live and die for such doctrines. May we learn this lesson well at the feet of this patristic giant.

Michael A. G. Haykin

---

6.   Athanasius, *To the Bishops of Egypt* 21, italics added, translation mine.

7.   Gregory of Nazianzus, *Oration* 45.4.

1

'THE DIVINE POWER HAS RAISED YOU UP TO BE AS *CONTRA MUNDUM*':

Life in Alexandria during the Diocletian Persecution and the Rise of Constantine

Introduction

On 26 February 1791, four days before he died, John Wesley wrote to encourage the young Member of Parliament, William Wilberforce, in his stand against the slave trade:

> Unless the divine power has raised you up to be as *Athanasius contra mundum*, I see not how you can go through your glorious enterprise, in opposing that execrable villainy, which is the scandal of religion, of England, and of human nature. Unless God has raised you up for this very thing, you will be worn out by the opposition of men and devils. But 'if God be for you, who can be against you?' Are all of them together stronger than God? O 'be not weary in well doing!' Go on, in the name of God and in the power of his might, till even American slavery (the vilest that ever saw the sun) shall vanish away before it.[1]

Wesley was seeking to inspire Wilberforce with the example of Athanasius, the bishop of Alexandria from 328 to 373. Five times the bishop was exiled, living a total of seventeen years away from his congregation and diocese, all for his clear-headed defence of the doctrine of the deity of Christ. 'In all of Christian history,

---

1.   John Wesley, *Works*, vol. XIII, Letters, 3rd ed. (Grand Rapids, MI: Baker Books, 1986), p. 153.

it is safe to say, few churchmen have been so entirely embroiled
in doctrinal and ecclesiastical disputes as Athanasius.'[2] So writes
Patrick Henry Reardon in a statement that few would contest.
Athanasius has become famous as the one who almost single-
handedly defended Nicene orthodoxy; it was indeed a case of
Athanasius *contra mundum*. Hans von Campenhausen writes of
him: 'The whole subsequent development of the Greek-Byzantine
Imperial Church was based on the struggle and success of this
one man.'[3] Athanasius's name derives, appropriately enough,
from the Greek word for 'immortal' or 'no death'. He was born,
lived, and died in Alexandria, but as the patriarch of Alexandria,
while in exile, he saw a fair portion of the known world–his
first two exiles were in the West (335-337 and 339-346) but his
last three were in the Egyptian desert (356-362, 362-363, and
365-366). In a sense, he spent his life battling emperors and
heretics, but he did not live by controversy alone. It is, therefore,
a little misleading to call him, as Carl Beckwith does, 'something
of a one-issue man'.[4]

Alexandrian church and society

Alexandria in Egypt was one of the finest cities of the ancient
world, renowned as a city of culture and scholarship. It was
also renowned as a city of rebellion against imperial authority.[5]
Being located at the western end of the Nile Delta, it almost
served as the gateway to Egypt–the doorway into it rather than
the center of it. It was also a major port, like a frog overlooking
a pond, as Plato described many Greek cities of the ancient

2. Patrick Henry Reardon, 'Athanasius: Pugnacious Defender of Orthodoxy,'
    Christian History 85 (2005), p. 33.

3. Hans von Campenhausen, *The Fathers of the Greek Church* (London: A. & C. Black,
    1963), pp. 70-71.

4. Carl Beckwith, 'Athanasius,' in *Shapers of Christian Orthodoxy*, ed. Bradley G. Green
    (Nottingham: Apollos, 2010), p. 166.

5. Christopher Haas, *Alexandria in Late Antiquity* (London: The John Hopkins
    University Press, 1997), pp. 6-11.

world.[6] E. R. Hardy's comment is apt: 'Alexandria was the capital and gateway of Roman Egypt without being quite part of the country.'[7] And as Christopher Haas writes: 'Even today Alexandrians speak of traveling "to Egypt".'[8]

Unlike Athens and Rome, Alexandria had been planned. Its site had been selected by Alexander the Great, who also gave it its name. It was nearly five miles in length and one mile in width, with main streets over 100 feet wide. Its harbor was dominated by its 400-foot lighthouse Pharos—taller than the Statue of Liberty.[9] Pharos was one of the Seven Wonders of the World until it was destroyed by a series of earthquakes over the centuries, and collapsed finally in 1303. Being situated just west of the Nile Delta, Alexandria did not experience the annual floods to the same extent as did towns within the Delta. Every August and September the Nile would flood, and fill the wells and conduits of the city. However, the water was not fit to drink until the silt and rubbish had settled, which was about November.[10] Out of necessity, Alexandria was a city of cisterns, linked by a system of conduits leading into them. Indeed, Julius Caesar was almost defeated at Alexandria in 48-47 B.C. because the locals poisoned the cisterns.[11]

Alexandria possessed a growing Christian population by the time of Athanasius. According to Epiphanius, there were nine churches within the city.[12] Christopher Haas says that there were probably sixteen presbyters, which could mean about a dozen individual parishes.[13] So far as the general population is

---

6.   Plato, *Phaedo*, 109B.

7.   E. R. Hardy, *Christian Egypt* (New York: Oxford University Press, 1952), p. 6.

8.   Haas, *Alexandria in Late Antiquity*, p. 33.

9.   Haas, *Alexandria in Late Antiquity*, p. 25; Jean-Yves Empereur, *Alexandria Rediscovered* (London: British Museum Press, 1998), p. 56.

10.   Empereur, *Alexandria Rediscovered*, pp. 131, 134.

11.   Ibid., pp. 125-30.

12   Athanasius, *Select Works and Letters* (NPNF[2] 4:243, n.6).

13.   See Haas, *Alexandria in Late Antiquity*, p. 212.

concerned, Alexandria was second only to Rome in the ancient world. Estimates of the population vary from about 200,000[14] to about 400,000 inhabitants,[15] but even this higher figure may be an underestimate. Perhaps double that number of souls lived there, with about a quarter of the population being Jewish. It bears noting that Christopher Haas sees urban society in Alexandria in late antiquity as 'fundamentally two-tiered,' with no real 'middle class'.[16]

Egypt itself had consisted of three provinces since the days before the emperor Hadrian (reigned A.D. 117-138). Hadrian made four, but Athanasius speaks of three.[17] Restructuring was popular in the late third and early fourth century, but mostly a tripartite structure prevailed: the East Delta and Heptanomia; Aegyptus the Central and West Delta; and the Thebaid in the south.[18] By the year 320, there were about ninety to a hundred bishoprics in Egypt, including Libya and the Pentapolis, to the west.[19]

As for the city of Alexandria, Philo, who lived there from about 20 B.C. - A.D. 50, writes of five districts, but two were apparently called the quarters of the Jews.[20] By the time of Athanasius, there were three distinct sectors: the Egyptian sector in the southwest with the magnificent Temple of Serapis (where the sacred bull was sacrificed until the temple was destroyed in 391); the Hellenic district with its celebrated library; and the Jewish sector in the east. It was also the great granary of the Roman Empire. Plutarch called it 'a nursing mother for men

---

14. Ibid., pp. 45-47.

15. Empereur, *Alexandria Rediscovered*, p. 195.

16. Haas, *Alexandria in Late Antiquity*, p. 51.

17. Athanasius, *Defence Before Constantius* 32.

18. See Roger S. Bagnall, *Egypt in Late Antiquity* (Princeton, NJ: Princeton University Press, 1993), pp. 63-64 for details.

19. Ibid., p. 285.

20. Philo, *Flaccus* 55; see also Haas, *Alexandria in Late Antiquity*, pp. 47-48.

of every nation'.[21] Dio Chrysostom in the second century referred to Alexandria as 'the crossroads of the world, serving it as a market place serves a single city'.[22] For centuries it was the agricultural capital of the Roman Empire.

The pagan historian, Ammianus Marcellinus, praised Alexandria as 'the crown of all cities'[23]— although he may have been only referring to all of the cities in Egypt. It was a city of apparent contrasts. Like Carthage in Augustine's day, it was seen as a place of temptation, full of baths and taverns.[24] It was also the home of intellectual and philosophical pursuits, the home of Archimedes, Euclid, and Philo, as well as Clement (c.150–215) and Origen (c.185–254), two of the most influential theologian/philosophers in the early church.

Christianity is supposed to have been brought to Alexandria by Mark, the author of the second Gospel. He is said to have entered through one of the city gates, but a strap on one of his sandals broke. He naturally took the sandal to a nearby cobbler, but the cobbler managed to injure himself with his awl, and cried out, 'God is one!' Mark did the Christ-like thing of spitting on the ground, making some clay, and applying it to the cobbler's injured hand. There was immediate healing, and the cobbler, Annianus and his household were soon converted. Indeed, Annianus became Mark's successor as head of the Alexandrian Christian community.[25]

---

21.   Plutarch, *Life of Alexander* 26.

22.   Cited in Alvyn Pettersen, *Athanasius* (London: Geoffrey Chapman, 1995), p. 1.

23.   Ammianus Marcellinus, *The Later Roman Empire* (A.D.354–378), trans. by Walter Hamilton (London; Penguin, 2004), 22 16 (p. 252).

24.   See Haas, *Alexandria in Late Antiquity*, pp. 68–69; Thomas C. Oden, *The African Memory of Mark* (Downers Grove, IL: InterVarsity Press, 2011), pp. 144–145.

25.   *History of the Patriarchs of the Coptic Church of Alexandria*, trans. by B. Evetts, Part I, chapter 2 (http://www.tertullian.org/fathers/severus_hermopolis_hist_alex_patr_01_part1.htm#CHAPTER_II).

The Great Persecution (303–313)

In 284, Diocletian, a conservative pagan, came to the imperial throne. He tried desperately to rescue the empire from the succession of thuggish generals who had seized the crown of Caesar in the third century and ruled—or misruled—the empire. *Peace Everywhere* (*Ubique Pax*) was the motto on Roman coins, but it was the peace of conquest and pagan unity. To approach Diocletian, one had to address him as 'Lord' (*dominus*), prostrate oneself three times, not make eye contact, and kiss the hem of his purple robe.

By 293, there were four men of power who were ruling the empire—Diocletian was the Augustus in the East (his palace was at Nicomedia in Bithynia), with Galerius as his Caesar, while Maximian was the Augustus in the West, with Constantius as his Caesar. All four men wore the imperial purple. For a time the decay of the empire seemed to be arrested, and perhaps even reversed. This did not appear to bode well for the Christians. It was still the Roman Empire, but, in the words of Peter Leithart, 'Milan in Italy, Trier and Arles in Gaul, Serdica, Sirmium, and Thessalonica in the Balkans became every bit as much capitals as Rome itself.'[26] A huge empire can be intimidating but it can also become ponderous.

Haruspices were priests who claimed mastery over the art of divining the future by examining the entrails of sacrificed animals. After 299 the god Apollo was silent, and 'profane men' were blamed—a charge that could easily be laid at the door of Christians. Diocletian ordered all members of the imperial court to sacrifice to the gods. Then the army had to follow suit. In 302, leaders of the dualistic cult of Mani were burnt, along with their scriptures, as, in Diocletian's view, 'it is wrong to ... desert the ancient religion for some new one'.[27] The Christians were next in the firing line. What antagonised Diocletian about

26.   Peter J. Leithart, *Defending Constantine* (Downers Grove, IL: IVP, 2010), pp. 38–39.

27.   Cited in Leithart, *Defending Constantine*, p. 17.

Christians was their exclusivism—their refusal to respect other people's gods. Even the philosophical Porphyry, an apostate Christian, called for the execution of unrepentant Christians.

In 302, a deacon named Romanus burst into the emperor's palace in Antioch and denounced corrupt pagan rituals. It was a brave but reckless act. His tongue was cut out on Diocletian's orders, he was tortured and then executed. Inclusivism, whether ancient or modern, is a doctrine which can have savage implications. So began the Great Persecution, from 303 to 311. On 23 February 303, Diocletian and Galerius banned Christian worship, ordered Christian sacred books to be burned, and decreed that no one could use the law courts unless he had first sacrificed to the gods. There was no fixed penalty for disobedience; it was up to the local officials. The second edict compelled clergy to sacrifice. People were maimed for life by being put on the rack, or they were scorched on gridirons. Eyes were gouged out, limbs hacked off, sexual organs cut off, and noses slit. By the time of the fourth edict, it was a case of sacrifice or die. The Great Persecution was particularly severe in the East, and especially in Egypt.[28]

By 305 Diocletian was both ageing and ailing, so he took the unprecedented step of abdicating in the East, in order to grow prize cabbages in his palace in Split, now part of Croatia. Galerius and Constantius became the Augusti, and Severus and Maximin the Caesars. Maximian in the West also retired, for a time at least. However, Constantius died in York nearly a year later in 306 — his persecution of Christians had never amounted to much more than demolishing some church buildings; and his son, Constantine, who had been with Galerius in the East, escaped and fled westwards to be acclaimed as Augustus by the army of Britain. Eventually, four Augusti were recognised — Galerius, Licinius, Constantine, and Maximin. In addition, there were two usurpers, Maxentius

---

28. For the Great Persecution, see W. H. C. Frend, *Martyrdom and Persecution in the Early Church* (Oxford: Basil Blackwell, 1965), pp. 476-535. For Egypt, see Eusebius, *Church History* 8.7-11.

(Maximian's son) and Alexander. Even at this stage, Constantine was most reluctant to impose the imperial religious policy. In fact, he restored what had been taken from the Christians.

Maxentius ruled over Spain until it rebelled and recognised Constantine, who thus became Augustus of Britain, Gaul, and Spain. Constantine also put down the forces of the aged rebel, Maximian, who had come out of retirement. In 311, at the end of his life, Galerius issued an edict of toleration before dying in great pain. This left Maximin to occupy the Asiatic dominions and to continue the persecution of Christians, and Licinius to occupy the European dominions. Maxentius remained a contender for the throne.

Just outside Rome, at the Milvian Bridge, on 28 October 312, Constantine defeated Maxentius. It was a momentous victory. The Sibylline Oracles had told Maxentius—with convenient ambiguity—that the enemy of the Romans would die that day,[29] but it was Maxentius who was drowned. According to Lactantius, Constantine had received a vision to mark 'the heavenly sign of God'—the Chi-Rho symbol, denoting the first two letters in the Greek word for Christ—on his soldiers' shields before the battle. So confident was Constantine of divine favor that he confronted Maxentius with only a quarter of his troops.

So it was that in 312 Constantine professed conversion to the Christian faith. Timothy Barnes does not see him as ill-educated,[30] but he could be bombastic and reckless. W. H. C. Frend is probably a little harsh in referring to his 'overweening ambition',[31] but it was not for nothing that his army colleagues nicknamed him 'Bullneck'. Ambiguities abound in life. Physically, Constantine was tall and athletic, but he also possessed a violent temper.

---

29. Timothy Barnes, *Constantine and Eusebius* (Cambridge, MA: Harvard University Press, 1981), pp. 41-43

30. Ibid., p. 73.

31. W. H. C. Frend, *The Rise of Christianity* (London: Darton, Longman and Todd, 1984), p. 475.

According to A. H. M. Jones, Constantine was 'in some sense converted to Christianity in the year 312'.[32] Jones does not paint Constantine's conversion as a spiritual experience but contends that it did lead to his ultimate and genuine adoption of the Christian faith.[33] Others have been less favourable, with Leo Tolstoy calling Constantine 'the heathen of heathens, whom the Church has canonized for all his vice and crimes'.[34] Tolstoy especially objected to church councils and metaphysics. More sympathetic is the estimate of Norman Baynes, that the emperor 'definitely identified himself with Christianity, with the Christian church and the Christian creed'.[35] And Timothy Barnes notes, 'After 28 October 312 the emperor consistently thought of himself as God's servant, entrusted with a divine mission to convert the Roman Empire to Christianity.'[36]

The debate as to whether or not Constantine became a genuine Christian is not our immediate concern. Certainly, in 312 there were many reasons for an emperor, or anybody else for that matter, not to identify with the Christian Church. The senatorial aristocracy of Rome, the higher grades of the civil service, and army officers were predominantly pagan. To cite A. H. M. Jones: 'The goodwill of the Christians was hardly worth gaining.'[37] This may be somewhat overdone, but rather more so is Timothy Barnes's contention that 'Christianity was powerful and respectable long before it acquired an imperial champion.'[38] Barnes seems to have forgotten that Constantine professed conversion in the twilight of the Great Persecution.

32. A. H. M. Jones, *Constantine and the Conversion of Europe* (Harmondsworth, Middlesex: Penguin, 1949), p. 85.

33. Ibid., p. 105.

34. Leo Tolstoy, *What I Believe*, trans. Constantine Popoff (London: Elliot Stock, 1885), p. 204.

35. N. H. Baynes, *Constantine the Great and the Christian Church* (London: H. Milford, 1929), p. 29.

36. Barnes, *Constantine and Eusebius*, pp. 43 and 275.

37. Jones, *Constantine and the Conversion of Europe*, p. 85.

38. Barnes, *Constantine and Eusebius*, p. 191.

For better or for worse, Constantine saw himself as the imperial protector of the church, which meant that he was not loath to interfere in the church's internal affairs. To the Persian king, Sapor, Constantine wrote: 'I am convinced that the greatest safety and prosperity will be enjoyed everywhere when God through the pure and righteous worship of the Christians and from their agreement concerning the divinity shall deign to draw all men unto Himself.'[39] He became scornful of the pagans: 'Let them have if they wish their temple of lies. We have the glorious edifice of the truth.'[40]

By 312–313, Constantine was subsidising the Catholic Church from public funds and Christian clergy were released from public burdens. On 29 October 312, after he had entered Rome, Constantine declined to ascend the Capitol to perform the customary sacrifices and to give thanks to Jupiter. At the same time, the head of Maxentius was paraded through the streets of Rome to overawe all potential opposition.

In 313 Maximin attacked Licinius but was defeated. Licinius then came out with the Edict of Milan, which favoured freedom of worship. Licinius and Constantine were lauded as 'the champions of peace and piety'. Maximin, the persecutor of Christians, professed to see the error of his ways and committed suicide. Licinius had killed off potential rivals and took to persecuting Christians until Constantine defeated him in 324, and had him executed. Constantine moved the capital from Nicomedia to Byzantium, which later he named, not surprisingly, Constantinople.

Constantine and the Christian faith

Constantine's policy was decidedly pro-Christian in a number of ways. An African Christian, suitably named Africanus, was appointed to tutor Constantine's eldest son. For the next five years, the mints of Constantine continued to issue coins in

39. Baynes, *Constantine the Great and the Christian Church*, pp. 26–27.

40. Frend, *The Rise of Christianity*, p. 496.

honor of Hercules, Mars, Jupiter and the Unconquered Sun, but Timothy Barnes is probably right to dismiss this as 'the dead weight of iconographic tradition'.[41] More significant is the fact that imperial rhetoricians refused to use pagan references in their panegyrics to him. Also, the shields in Constantine's army portrayed a cross-like symbol. Laws were passed which favored the church and her teachings. For example, in 320 Constantine repealed Augustus's laws against celibacy and childless marriages, while in 321 bequests to the church were legalised, and manumissions (the freeing of slaves) before bishops became valid.[42] Lavish churches were built at public expense. He directed Alexander, the bishop of Alexandria, to transfer the sacred cubit from the temple of Serapis (the Greek-Egyptian god who was worshipped as a man by the Greeks or as a bull by the Egyptians) to the church. Pagans argued that this could have disastrous consequences in that the Nile River would not overflow. It did, however, and the Christian cause was strengthened.[43] In 325 gladiatorial shows were prohibited, although enforcing the ban proved ineffective in the West. Sunday was recognised as a holiday. This was not a shift from Saturday but recognition of what Christians had practiced for centuries. Crucifixion and branding on the face were forbidden, but not the forcing of a criminal to drink boiling oil or molten lead. Ironically enough, considering Constantine's own marital situation—he had divorced Minervina to marry Fausta—divorce laws were tightened.[44]

Constantine had not reigned in Rome for six months before the Donatist controversy broke out in North Africa.[45]

---

41. Barnes, *Constantine and Eusebius*, p. 48.

42. Frend, *The Rise of Christianity*, pp. 487–490.

43. Socrates, *Church History* 1.18.

44. Frend, *The Rise of Christianity*, pp. 487–88.

45. For the Donatists, see W. H. C. Frend, *The Donatist Church* (Oxford: Oxford University Press, 1951). However, the thesis that Donatism has an essentially social and national basis, rather than a religious one, is more than contentious.

The rigorist party of Majorinus (the Donatists) appealed to Constantine against the election of Caecilian as bishop of Carthage. Constantine convened a council, which upheld the claims of Caecilian, and in 314 another Western council, this time at Arles, confirmed what was done at Rome. From 316 to 321, Constantine sought to coerce the Donatists. As A. H. M. Jones comments: 'The Church had acquired a protector, but it had also acquired a master.'[46] His ardent and almost Erastian biographer, Eusebius of Caesarea, enthused of Constantine: 'He exercised a peculiar care over the church of God'.[47] The claim was that he prayed that all would become Christians, but compelled no one.[48] Inevitably, tolerance has its limits, and he sought to prohibit sacrifices and idol worship.

Peter, whom Epiphanius portrays as 'a kindly man',[49] was the bishop of Alexandria from 300 until his martyrdom under Maximinus in 311—hence he lived through the time of the Great Persecution. Difficulties arose in the diocese because Peter fled in 303 and again in 306. This left something of a vacuum in the diocese, and Melitius (often spelled Meletius), the bishop of Lycopolis, stepped in to undertake many of Peter's tasks. In Robert Archie Riall's view, Melitius 'represented the rigorist opposition to Peter's policy of clemency',[50] an interpretation endorsed by David Gwynn[51] and Peter Leithart.[52]

It is also possible that Melitius ordained Arius, although R. P. C. Hanson regards that as unlikely.[53] After Peter's second

---

46. Jones, *Constantine and the Conversion of Europe*, p. 125.

47. Eusebius, *The Life of Constantine* 1.44.

48. Ibid., 2.16.

49. Epiphanius, *Panarion* 68.3.1.

50. Robert Archie Riall, 'Athanasius Bishop of Alexandria: The Politics of Spirituality (Egypt)' (PhD dissertation, University of Cincinnati, 1987), p. 3.

51. David Gwynn, *Athanasius of Alexandria: Bishop, Theologian, Ascetic, Father*, Christian Theology in Context (Oxford: Oxford University Press, 2012), p. 23.

52. Peter Leithart, *Athanasius* (Grand Rapids: Baker, 2011), p. 1.

53. R. P. C. Hanson, *The Search for the Christian Doctrine of God: The Arian Controversy 318–381* (Edinburgh: T&T Clark, 1988), pp. 4–5.

exile, in 306, he returned to Alexandria and had Melitius excommunicated. We know little of the details of this time, and it must be admitted that the arch-heresy hunter, Epiphanius, treats Melitius with considerable generosity and sympathy.[54] Later Athanasius claimed that Melitius was excommunicated because he had offered sacrifice to idols, and committed other crimes,[55] and Socrates referred somewhat vaguely to his 'former disorderly conduct' and 'the rashness and levity of his character'.[56] C. Wilfred Griggs rejects these charges,[57] as does Rowan Williams who notes that 'Athanasius is never a fanatically accurate controversialist'.[58] In the midst of the Arian struggle, Athanasius might have made his prophetic reply to this, as he dismissed the Melitians as chameleons who had no idea of what Christianity is.[59]

The situation was rendered more difficult, in one sense at least, when Peter was beheaded as a martyr on 26 November 311. The Egyptian Church was severely divided, yet not as divided as the North African Church of Carthage where the Donatists confronted the Catholics (members of the Great Church), in almost equal numbers. In fact, Peter's martyrdom may have helped to keep the two groups together, or not so far apart, in Alexandria. It certainly meant that, if the Melitians were rigorists, their cause was not so convincing given that the Catholic bishop was a martyr for the faith.[60]

---

54. See Epiphanius, *Panarion* 68.

55. Athanasius, *Defence Against the Arians* 59; Socrates, *Church History* 1.6.

56. Socrates, *Church History* 1.9.

57. C. Wilfred Griggs, *Early Egyptian Christianity from its Origins to 451 C.E.*, Coptic Studies 2 (Leiden: Brill, 1988), p, 117.

58. Rowan Williams, *Arius: Heresy and Tradition* (London: Darton, Longman and Todd, 1987), p. 36.

59. Athanasius, *History of the Arians* 78–80.

60. 'Catholic' here is used in the original sense of this word, namely 'universal.'

The early life of Athanasius

Such was the background and something of the world into which Athanasius was born and in which he grew up. Persecution had given way to imperial favor. The church, having undergone the fires of persecution for centuries, now had to live in a new world and confront a new set of problems. During the first three centuries of her existence, the church faced coercion from without; in the fourth century, she suddenly faced a world, which was professedly friendlier to the gospel. Yet it was not a case of paradise regained on earth. As external pressures eased, internal pressures increased.

Strangely enough, we have no contemporary record of Athanasius's life. For such a prolific author, Athanasius left surprisingly little in terms of biographical information. In contrast to Augustine of Hippo, Athanasius left no *Confessions* to record his inner life, and he was somewhat reluctant to talk about personal matters. His name, however, became a household one and was increasingly used by parents in Egypt to name their children as the fourth century wore on.[61] Physically, he seems to have been hardly imposing, unlike the tall and slender Arius, although he may have had red hair. Indeed, he has been described as 'almost childlike in size'.[62] Julian was to later mock him as a diminutive figure.[63] With the imaginative touch of a novelist, rather than an historian, E. M. Forster describes Athanasius: 'Physically he was blackish, but active and strong. One recognizes a modern street type.'[64] Justo González seems to be behind the modern myth that Athanasius's enemies had dubbed him 'the black dwarf'.[65] In later iconography of

61.   Riall, 'Athanasius Bishop of Alexandria,' p. 350.

62.   Richard Rubenstein, *When Jesus Became God* (New York: Harcourt Brace, 1999), p. 62.

63.   See William Bright, 'Athanasius' in *A Dictionary of Christian Biography*, eds. William Smith and Henry Wace (London: John Murray, Albemarle Street, 1877), p. 182.

64.   E. M. Forster, *Pharos and Pharillon* (London: Hogarth Press, 1961), p. 48.

65.   Justo González, *The Story of Christianity* (Peabody, MA: Prince Press edition, 1999),

the Eastern Orthodox Churches, Athanasius is portrayed like every other Eastern Church Father. Quite intentionally, the Orthodox Churches portray them all in the same way, implying that their messages too are identical, and constitute in fact one unchangeable message.

Athanasius was apparently born in Alexandria, but, if he ever mastered Coptic, which admittedly was only a recent invention, from the third century,[66] he may have only done so during his third and fourth exiles, in 356-362 and 362-363. Riall believes that he was a Greek speaker, and so only ever used interpreters,[67] although W. H. C. Frend believes that he was also able to preach in the Coptic language.[68] During his first two exiles in the West, which took up some nine years of his life, it is not unlikely that he learnt Latin. It is not known whether his parents were Christians. Richard Rubenstein asserts that they were 'very likely pagans'.[69] Gregory of Nazianzus, in his oration on Athanasius after his death, stated: 'He was brought up, from the first, in religious habits and practices.'[70] Athanasius's aunt was later to be denied burial in the church cemetery, presumably because she supported her nephew.[71] But that may not tell us much. Very sensibly, David Gwynn is content to be indefinite, and simply to comment that Athanasius possibly had Christian parents.[72]

As we have seen, the name 'Athanasius' presumably comes from '*a-thanatos*', meaning 'without death'. That may point to a Christian upbringing, although that is not certain. The *History*

p. 173. The description is repeated in Gerald R. McDermott, *The Great Theologians: A Brief Guide* (Downers Grove, Il: IVP, 2010), p. 30.

66. See Bagnall, *Egypt in Late Antiquity*, p. 238.

67. Riall, 'Athanasius Bishop of Alexandria,' pp. 358-362.

68. W. H. C. Frend, 'Athanasius as an Egyptian Christian Leader in the Fourth Century' in *Religion Popular and Unpopular in the Early Christian Centuries* (London: Variorum Reprints, 1976), p. 33.

69. Rubenstein, *When Jesus Became God*, p. 104.

70. Gregory of Nazianzus, *Oration 21* (NPNF² 7:6).

71. Athanasius, *History of the Arians* 13.

72. Gwynn, *Athanasius of Alexandria*, p. 2.

of the Patriarchs of the Coptic Church of Alexandria says that he was raised by his pagan, widowed mother who did her best to entice women to seduce him,[73] but there is abundant reason not to regard this as a highly reliable source. Sozomen writes of Athanasius as self-taught, eloquent, and intelligent.[74] That much can be accepted without dispute. W. H. C. Frend writes of Athanasius's 'Alexandrian middle-class background'[75] but Timothy Barnes writes of his 'low-class origin'.[76] Robert Riall adds to the uncertainty: 'Athanasius was from an Alexandrian Christian family of moderate standing.'[77] Since Athanasius, in his later exiles, occasionally hid in the tombs of his ancestors, that may indicate a certain level of wealth.[78] His enemies accused him of being 'a rich man, and powerful, and able to do anything',[79] but Athanasius portrayed himself as a poor man, or at least an ascetic one.

Athanasius seems to say that he has no recollection of Maximian's persecution of A.D. 303. His actual words in his *History of the Arians* are:

> I have heard from our fathers, and I believe their report to be a faithful one, that long ago, when a persecution arose in the time of Maximian, the grandfather of Constantius, the Gentiles concealed our brethren the Christians, who were sought after, and frequently suffered the loss of their own substance, and had trial of imprisonment, solely that they might not betray the fugitives.[80]

---

73. *History of the Patriarchs of the Coptic Church of Alexandria*, trans. by B. Evetts, Part I, chapter 8 (http://www.tertullian.org/fathers/severus_hermopolis_hist_alex_patr_02_part2.htm#ATHANASIUS_I) .

74. Sozomen, *Church History* 2.17.

75. Frend, 'Athanasius as an Egyptian Christian Leader,' p. 21, n.1.

76. Barnes, *Athanasius and Constantius*, p. 14, p. 244, n.42.

77. Riall, 'Athanasius Bishop of Alexandria,' p. 13.

78. Sozomen, *Church History* 6.12.

79. Athanasius, *Defence Against the Arians* 9.

80. Athanasius, *History of the Arians* 64.

Defying this testimony, Hans von Campenhausen considers that Athanasius did experience and remember the persecutions.[81] Athanasius's comment also reveals part of the reason for the failure of the Great Persecution: Christians had been around long enough to have become a respected part of society. The fourth century was to see a Christian community, and notably, its clergy, increase in political and social influence.[82]

When he became bishop of Alexandria, Athanasius was still regarded as a young man. The previous bishop was Alexander, who is described by Rufinus as 'quiet and gentle',[83] and one who claimed authority over nearly a hundred bishops. It is usually contended that Athanasius was born somewhere about A.D. 296,[84] 297,[85] or 299, in Timothy Barnes's view, which seems more probable.[86] Socrates cites a story from Rufinus about a game of acting as a bishop, which young Athanasius was playing when Alexander saw him. Alexander was so impressed that he did not re-baptize the children whom Athanasius had 'baptized'. Socrates himself regarded this as not improbable,[87] but it is usually rejected today as unhistorical.[88] If Alexander came to the episcopal chair in 313, Athanasius may have been about fourteen or fifteen years of age, which many have regarded as somewhat too old to have been playing games of 'bishop'. The marriageable age for young girls at this time was, after all, twelve.

81. Von Campenhausen, *Fathers of the Greek Church*, p. 69.

82. See E. A. Judge and S. R. Pickering, 'Papyrus Documentation of Church and Community in Egypt to the Mid-Fourth Century,' *Jahrbuch für Antike und Christentum* 20, no. 1 (1977): pp. 47–71.

83. Cited in Frances Young, *From Nicaea to Chalcedon* (London: SCM, 1983), p. 58.

84. E.g. Thomas G. Weinandy, *Athanasius: A Theological Evaluation* (Aldershot: Ashgate, 2007), p. 1; Bright, 'Athanasius,' p. 179; even by George D. Dragas, *Saint Athanasius of Alexandria: Original Research and New Perspectives* (Rollinsford, NH: Orthodox Research Institute, 2005), pp. 192–93.

85. Hanson, *Search for the Christian Doctrine*, pp. 246–247.

86. Barnes, *Athanasius and Constantius*, p. 10.

87. Socrates, *Church History* 1.15.

88. E.g. Riall, 'Athanasius Bishop of Alexandria,' p. 353; Bright, 'Athanasius,' p. 180.

2

'HIS WORD AND HIS WISDOM MUST BE EVERLASTING':

Development of Early Christology and the Way to Nicaea

Pre-Nicene Christology and the Concern for Christological Orthodoxy

The clash between Athanasius and Arius was not one between two titans. There were many variations within Arianism, and Arius himself can barely be regarded as the leader of a party comparable to Athanasius's role in standing for Nicene orthodoxy. First of all, however, there is a need to review, albeit briefly, the question of how the person of Christ was understood before Nicaea. Athanasius contended that the church had always clearly adhered to the full deity of Christ, and so asked: 'But you, O modern Jews and disciples of Caiaphas, how many fathers can you assign to your phrases?'[1] He considered, 'even before Nicaea that heresy was held in detestation'.[2] Thomas Weinandy is one of many in maintaining that prior to Nicaea, 'There was a hierarchical conception within the Trinity.'[3] R. P. C. Hanson goes much further and contends that before Nicaea there was no orthodox view of Christ's person, but this is untenable.[4]

1. Athanasius, *Defence of the Nicene Definition* 27.

2. Athanasius, *Councils of Ariminum and Seleucia* 20.

3. Thomas G. Weinandy, *Athanasius: A Theological Evaluation* (Aldershot: Ashgate, 2007), p. 50.

4. R. P. C. Hanson, *The Search for the Christian Doctrine of God: The Arian Controversy 318–381* (Edinburgh: T&T Clark, 1988), pp. xvii-xx.

It has become fashionable for historians to claim that Arianism was not obviously heretical at this stage, for the issue of Christ's deity was a genuinely undecided one even after Nicaea.[5] David Gwynn asserts, 'In the period in which he wrote Athanasius's doctrinal position was certainly not the traditional and universal faith of the Church that he wished to claim'.[6] He castigates him for referring to his enemies as Arians, and accuses him of constructing 'an entirely artificial polarization'.[7] Gwynn, however, admits that he has no solution as to what to call Athanasius's opponents, whether Arian, Eusebian, or Lucianist.[8] Athanasius was not writing a thesis on 'The Development of Eastern Christology in the Aftermath of Nicaea,' but struggling for the church's recognition of the full deity of her Savior.

Rowan Williams sees Arius as an academic (in the Platonic sense but with overtones of being something of a charismatic freewheeler), in a situation which increasingly called for a tidy Catholic solution.[9] Not surprisingly, Williams portrays Arius as a thinker and exegete of resourcefulness, sharpness, and originality.[10] Certainly, there was some doctrinal and disciplinary untidiness possible in the third century. For example, Cyprian of Carthage and Stephen of Rome rancorously disputed over whether schismatic or heretical baptism in the name of the Trinity was valid and hence unrepeatable. Baptism, in Cyprian's view, 'cannot be among heretics, because it can neither be separated

---

5. E.g. Colm Luibhéid, *The Council of Nicaea* (Ireland: Galway University Press, 1982), pp. 3 and 6; Richard Rubenstein, *When Jesus Became God* (New York: Harcourt Brace, 1999), pp. 9–10.

6. David M. Gwynn, *The Eusebians: The Polemic of Athanasius of Alexandria and the Construction of the 'Arian Controversy'*, Oxford Theological Monographs (Oxford: Oxford University Press, 2007), p. 170.

7. Ibid., p. 229.

8. Ibid., p. 228.

9. Rowan Williams, *Arius: Heresy and Tradition* (London: Darton, Longman and Todd, 1987), pp. 86–87.

10. Ibid., p. 116.

from the church nor from the Holy Spirit'.[11] To Stephen, and much later, Augustine, schismatic baptism was valid and not to be repeated, albeit not efficacious. Such a lack of precision became inappropriate in the fourth century. Sozomen, however, writes that Arius 'dared to preach in church what no one before him had ever suggested'.[12]

Geza Vermes has put forward what has been regarded as gospel truth in many circles, that the Jesus of history was 'the Jewish charismatic messenger of God', but by the early fourth century had come to be worshipped as the Lord of glory.[13] Yet from New Testament times, Christians have viewed God in triadic terms. The New Testament sets forth the mystery of 'the crucified God'—there is only one God, nevertheless Jesus Christ the man is Lord, with all authority in heaven and on earth, and the name which is above every name (Matthew 28:18; Philippians 2:10-11).[14] Still, we only recognise this when the Holy Spirit brings us to see what before was obscure to us. After the New Testament period, Christians sought to express this truth in gospel summaries. Hence Polycarp of Smyrna, as he was about to be burnt as a martyr, possibly in 155 or 156, prayed to the God of truth: 'For this reason, indeed for all things, I praise You, I bless You, I glorify You; through the eternal and heavenly high priest, Jesus Christ, Your beloved Son, through whom be glory to You, with Him and the Holy Spirit, both now and for the ages to come. Amen.'[15] Irenaeus of Lyon explained the deity of Christ in this way: 'So then the Father is Lord and the Son is Lord, and the Father is God and the Son is God; for that

---

11.   Cyprian, *Epistle* 73 (ANF 5:387).

12.   Sozomen, *Church History* 1.15.

13.   Geza Vermes, *Christian Beginnings from Nazareth to Nicaea, A.D.30–325* (London: Allen Lane, 2012), p. 242.

14.   See, for example, Richard Bauckham, *God Crucified: Monotheism and Christology in the New Testament* (Grand Rapids, MI: Eerdmans, 1998).

15.   *The Martyrdom of Polycarp* 14.

which is begotten of God is God.'[16] Tertullian, who was probably a layman in the legal profession, was the first to use the word 'Trinity'. He could speak of Jesus as 'in one Person at once God and man'.[17]

It is true that many of the early Fathers, notably Origen, had taught that Jesus was subordinate to the Father. Origen could be both complex and confusing. He wrote of the Father alone as the true God, and 'Whatever there is besides this God per se is constituted God by participation in his divinity.'[18] He was also not keen on Christians praying to the Son. Eusebius of Caesarea, the fourth-century author, too wrote: 'God willed to be a Father of a Son and he established a second light, one similar to himself in every respect.'[19] Yet he added: 'The generation of the Son is one thing, the creation through the Son another.'[20] Quite remarkably, Origen managed to influence both sides in the Arian controversy, as he warned: 'Let him who assigns a beginning to the Word of God or the wisdom of God beware lest he utters impiety against the unbegotten Father himself, in denying that he was always a Father.'[21] In fact, according to Origen, 'the omnipotence of Father and Son is one and the same'.[22]

Athanasius himself was forced to defend Dionysius of Alexandria, a bishop from 233–265, who in a dispute with his namesake, Dionysius of Rome, argued that the Son was distinct from the Father. As Caiaphas had denied Christ and appealed to Abraham, so, said Athanasius, the Arians deny Christ and appeal to Dionysius.[23] Dionysius was writing against the Sabellians of

16. Irenaeus, *Apostolic Preaching* 47.

17. Cited in J. N. D. Kelly, *Early Christian Doctrines*, 5th ed. (London: Adam and Charles Black, 1977), p. 151.

18. Luibhéid, *Council of Nicaea*, p. 48; Origen, *Commentary on John* 2.2.

19. Ibid., *p.* 58.

20. Ibid., 58; Hanson, *Search for the Christian Doctrine*, p. 51.

21. Origen, *On First Principles* I.II.3.

22. Ibid., I.II.10.

23. Athanasius, *On the Opinion of Dionysius* 3.

Pentapolis in Upper Libya, who viewed the Son and the Father as one divine person. To Athanasius, the Arians were ignoring biblical verses such as John 1:1 and 3, and Colossians 1:16, and, dishonestly and maliciously, hunting down stray expressions in Dionysius in order to bolster their own cause.[24] Athanasius regarded Sabellianism and Arianism as heresies, which fed off one another and were 'equal in impiety'.[25] It might be significant that both Sabellius and Arius seem to have come from Libya.[26]

Yet one of the earliest Fathers, Ignatius of Antioch (flourished 105–110), clearly taught that Christ is both begotten (*gennetos*) and unbegotten (*agennetos*): There is one physician, fleshly and spiritual, begotten and unbegotten, God in flesh, true life in death, of Mary and of God, passible and then impassible.[27] He used the surprising expression 'the blood of God',[28] and referred to Christ as 'son of a human and son of God'.[29] W. R. Schoedel is right to comment, somewhat too mildly one would think, that 'we have here the kernel of the later two-nature Christologies'.[30]

Taken as a whole, it is misleading to say that Arianism was ever regarded by the church as a viable form of Christianity, or that, as Richard Rubenstein thinks, early on in the dispute both sides treated each other as wrong and mistaken rather than evil and Satanic.[31] The Christian faith has always demanded a belief in Jesus as the resurrected Lord who would judge the whole world. What came to be called Arianism has always been regarded as a bridge not quite completed.

24. Ibid., 2, 4–5.

25. Ibid., 25.

26. For the claim that Sabellius was a Libyan, see Socrates, *Church History* 1.5.

27. William R. Schoedel, *Ignatius of Antioch*, Hermeneia (Philadelphia, PA: Fortress Press, 1985), pp. 60–62.

28. Schoedel, *Ignatius of Antioch*, pp. 40–42. See also his commentary sections on Ignatius, *Ephesians* 15.3; 18:2; Ignatius, *Romans* Preface, 3.3; 6.3; Ignatius, *Polycarp* 8.3.

29. Schoedel, *Ignatius of Antioch*, pp. 96–99.

30. Ibid., p. 60.

31. Rubenstein, *When Jesus Became God*, pp. 87–88.

Theological Conflict about Christ Prior to the
Council of Nicaea

Whatever the case, the aftermath of the Great Persecution saw the church beset by a controversy over the teaching of the Alexandrian presbyter, Arius (c.260–336). He was no fresh-faced clergyman hoping to make a name for himself but an experienced cleric, who pitted himself against what has become known as Trinitarian orthodoxy. In doing so, he precipitated what Rowan Williams has called 'the most dramatic internal struggle the Christian Church had so far experienced'.[32] Arius's writings have been lost—or destroyed, to be more precise—but it is doubtful that his opponents have misrepresented his views.[33] The situation is not, despite what Colm Luibhéid thinks, comparable to turning to Lenin to gain insight into the Tsars.[34]

There have been a number of interpretations of Arianism. In 1833 John Henry Newman saw the Antiochene school (such as Paul of Samosata and Lucian of Antioch) as standing behind Arius, while the Alexandrian school stood as the exemplar of traditional and revealed religion.[35] Joseph Lienhard thinks that Newman's book remains 'the elephant in the room',[36] while Lewis Ayres regards the Newman thesis as 'unsustainable'.[37] Christopher Stead too thinks the idea that Paul of Samosata was behind Arius is 'totally misconceived'.[38] Rather more severely, Stephen Thomas labels *The Arians of the Fourth Century* as 'Newman's first novel'.[39] Paradoxically, the great German

32. Williams, *Arius*, p. 1.

33. Contrary to Hanson, *Search for the Christian Doctrine*, p. 10.

34. Luibhéid, *The Council of Nicaea*, p. 17.

35. See John Henry Newman, *The Arians of the Fourth Century*, notes by Rowan Williams (Notre Dame, IN: University of Notre Dame Press, 2001).

36. Joseph T. Lienhard, S. J., 'From Gwatkin Onwards: A Guide through a Century and a Quarter of Studies on Arianism,' *Augustinian Studies* 44, no. 2 (2013): p. 267.

37. Cf. Ayres, *Nicaea and its Legacy*, p. 40, n.85.

38. C. Stead, 'Arius in Modern Research,' *Journal of Theological Studies* 45 (April 1994): p. 26.

39. Cited in Newman, *Arians of the Fourth Century*, p. xlvii.

exponent of liberalism, Adolf von Harnack, thought Arianism was practical polytheism, with two objects of worship, and that its triumph would have meant the end of authentic Christianity.[40] Following Albrecht Ritschl's elimination of metaphysics from theology, Harnack painted a general picture of growing Hellenistic dogma triumphing over the simple gospel.[41] Yet, he admired the resolute Alexandrian bishop: 'In the midst of all this Athanasius alone in the East stood like a rock in the sea.'[42]

H. M. Gwatkin viewed Arianism as heathen to the core, not as almost rationalistic as the Antiochenes were sometimes portrayed, nor as Jewish. He could praise Arius himself as a grave and blameless presbyter who wrestled with a real difficulty of the gospel, but added: 'The Arian Christ is nothing but a heathen idol invented to maintain a heathenish Supreme (Being) in heathen isolation from the world.'[43] G. L. Prestige saw it as 'one vast system of theological depravity'[44]—crypto-pagan, polytheistic, rationalistic, and a theology which rendered true salvation impossible. To Christopher Dawson, Arianism was 'a superficial rationalisation of Christianity'.[45] With considerable but perhaps not overwhelmingly compelling reason, Henry Chadwick sees Origen behind the views of Arius, and Irenaeus behind those of Athanasius.[46] Indeed, Timothy Barnes considers it neither necessary nor attractive to trace Arius's ideas to sources outside

---

40. Adolf von Harnack, *History of Dogma*, trans. Neil Buchanan (New York: Dover Publications, 1961), 4:43.

41. James Orr replied to this approach in *The Progress of Dogma* (1901).

42. Harnack, *History of Dogma*, 4:62.

43. H. M. Gwatkin, *The Arian Controversy* (1908 ed.; repr. Eugene, OR: Wipf and Stock, 2001), pp. 5–7.

44. G. L. Prestige, *Fathers and Heretics* (London: SPCK, 1948), p. 94.

45. Christopher Dawson, *The Making of Europe* (1932 ed.; repr. Washington, D.C.: The Catholic University of America Press, 2003), p. 46.

46. Henry Chadwick, *The Church in Ancient Society* (Oxford: Oxford University Press, 2003), p. 198. Khaled Anatolios also sees Athanasius continuing 'a distinctly Irenaean tradition' (Khaled Anatolios, *Athanasius: The Coherence of his Thought* [London: Routledge, 1998], pp. 23, 206).

the Christian tradition.[47] In fact, it is the view of C. Wilfred Griggs that 'the early decades of the controversy resemble a battle for power between two competing camps rather than a theological war'.[48] On balance, there is much to be said for Gerald Bray's view: 'Orthodoxy was *felt* before it was articulated, and it is more plausible to attribute the majority consensus to a genuine work of the Holy Spirit than it is to put it down to the machinations of clever individuals in positions of power.'[49]

As for Arius himself, Epiphanius tells us that Arius was born in Libya.[50] Two of his most determined episcopal supporters were also from Libya, Secundus and Theonas. Philostorgius, the pro-Arian historian, lists other Libyan bishops sympathetic to Arius,[51] and Rowan Williams claims that 'we know of no Libyan bishops opposing Arius'.[52] It is surely significant that in 331 or 332 Athanasius felt it necessary to conduct a pastoral visit to Libya, no doubt to shore up support. Arius had worked as a presbyter in Boukolia (or Baucalis), a region of herdsmen and shepherds, east of Alexandria, at the opposite end from the headquarters of the bishop, whether Alexander or Athanasius, at the western gate. Church buildings tended to appear on the edge of the city first, and only later, particularly with Athanasius, in the centre.

Epiphanius describes Arius as an old man at the time of the outbreak of the controversy, and in 333 Constantine, not far off death himself, described Arius's wasted and lifeless appearance. Because of these descriptions, some have placed Arius's birth in the 250s, but it is usually thought to have been a little later. Epiphanius's actual description of Arius is as follows: 'For the

---

47. Barnes, *Constantine and Eusebius*, p. 203.

48. C. Wilfred Griggs, *Early Egyptian Christianity from its Origins to 451 C.E.* (Leiden: Brill, 1988), p. 146.

49. Gerald Bray, *Creeds, Councils and Christ* (Leicester: IVP, 1984), p. 74.

50. Epiphanius, *Panarion* 69.1.2.

51. Philostorgius, *Church History* 1.8a; 7.6; 8.2.

52. Williams, *Arius*, p. 29.

old man, inflated with pride, departed from the true faith. He was well along in years and downcast in appearance, with the affectation of a cunning snake, able to steal away any guileless heart through his crafty pretence.'[53]

In a letter to Eusebius of Nicomedia, Arius called himself a 'fellow-Lucianist', which may mean he studied under the martyr Lucian of Antioch. Arius was ordained a presbyter by Achillas, Peter's successor at Alexandria, and was known as a respected cleric and ascetic. Sozomen claims that Arius was involved in the Meletian schism.[54] Melitius may have been a rigorist, but even this is uncertain. According to Sozomen, Peter excommunicated Melitius, but Arius objected and so was himself deposed. He then made his peace with Achillas after Peter's death and came to be ordained as a presbyter (he was already a deacon).[55] But Alexander, Athanasius, and Epiphanius do not mention any Arius-Melitius link at this time. Williams thinks that two men with the same name may have been identified as one,[56] since Arius was a common name. Timothy Barnes is also sceptical of Sozomen's account.[57] Not so W. H. C. Frend,[58] and it must be said that Sozomen is normally regarded as a reliable historian.[59]

Theodoret and Philostorgius think that Arius was an episcopal candidate in 313,[60] but Alexander was elected bishop of Alexandria. All this at a time when the church was also facing an unusually large number of problems: there was the Melitian schism; then Hieracas (or Hierax), who ran a monastery outside Leontopolis and, among other things, questioned the

53. Epiphanius, *Panarion* 69.3.1.
54. Sozomen, *Church History* 1.15.
55. Ibid., 1.15.
56. Williams, *Arius*, p. 39.
57. Barnes, *Constantine and Eusebius*, p. 202.
58. Frend, *Rise of Christianity*, p. 493.
59. See e.g. David Rohrbacher, *The Historians of Late Antiquity* (London: Routledge, 2002), p. 123.
60. Theodoret, *Church History* 1.1; Philostorgius, *Church History* 1.3.

resurrection of the body and the salvation of baptized infants; and Colluthus who appears to have been a Monarchian who viewed the three Persons of the Trinity as in fact one Person. Whatever the case, he was eventually reconciled to Alexander.

Writing in 1946, W. Telfer tried to argue that the Arian controversy did not break out until 323,[61] but the more usual, and, it must be said, more likely, date given is 318. It is true that Arian views spread fairly quickly. To cite Socrates: 'The evil which began in the Church at Alexandria, ran throughout all Egypt, Libya, and the upper Thebes, and at length diffused itself over the rest of the provinces and cities'.[62] What we have of Arius's teaching has survived in Athanasius's writings, not his own. In fact, only three texts can be directly ascribed to Arius:

a. His confession of faith to Alexander perhaps in 320 or 321 (found in Athanasius's *On the Councils of Ariminum and Seleucia* 16);

b. His letter to Eusebius of Nicomedia soon after this (found in Theodoret, *Church History* 1.4);

c. His confession (with Euzoïus) to the emperor in 327, or perhaps 333 or 335 (found in Socrates, *Church History* 1.26).[63]

In addition, Arius's *Thalia* ('Banquet') is given by Athanasius in *Against the Arians* 1.5-6 and *On the Councils of Ariminum and Seleucia* 15, where it is totally in poetic meter. Arius's profession, if it can be called by something so formal sounding, was given in the form of a jingle. Rowan Williams calls them 'dinner party songs'.[64] This kind of verse was popular in style and despised by

---

61. W. Telfer, 'When did the Arian Controversy Begin?', *Journal of Theological Studies* 47 (1946).

62. Socrates, *Church History* 1.6.

63. Ayres, *Nicaea and its Legacy*, p. 101, n.44. Ayres sees 327 as the most likely date.

64. R. Williams, 'Athanasius and the Arian Crisis,' in *The First Christian Theologians*, ed. G. R. Evans (Oxford: Blackwell, 2004), p. 161.

the educated classes.[65] Indeed, Athanasius mocked it as 'light and irreligious'[66] and having been written in 'an effeminate and ridiculous style'.[67]

God is said to pre-exist the Son: 'There was [a time] when he was not'[68] – a view of Christ that Athanasius described as like mud in a wallet.[69] Athanasius accused the Arians of deception in dropping the words 'a time', but they were trying to say that the Son of God was created before the creation of time in Genesis 1:1. God alone is 'without a beginning' (*anarchos*), while the Son has a beginning (*archē*). God alone is self-subsistent or *agennetos*. Arius complained: 'We are persecuted because we say that the Son had a beginning, but that God was without beginning.'[70] The Son, he argued, is 'a perfect creature of God, but not like other created objects'.[71] The Word is subject to change; only by grace can He be called 'God'.[72] Arius's key text was the Septuagint version of Proverbs 8:22, 'The Lord created me at the beginning of his ways, for his works.' To Athanasius, though, this verse described the creation of Jesus's body.[73] One of the other texts that Arius pointed to was Colossians 1:15, which describes Christ as 'the firstborn of all creation'. To Arius, this was understood not to mean that Christ is the ruler over all creation but was the first created being. To Athanasius, it was a title that indicated Christ's universal authority.

65. Barnes, *Constantine and Eusebius*, p. 205.

66. Athanasius, *Councils of Ariminum and Seleucia* 36.

67. Athanasius, *On the Opinion of Dionysius* 6. See also Athanasius, *Four Discourses Against the Arians* 1.2.

68. Athanasius, *Four Discourses Against the Arians* 1.13.

69. Ibid., 2.43.

70. Theodoret, *Church History* 1.4; Epiphanius, *Panarion* 69.6.7.

71. Cited in Barnes, *Constantine and Eusebius*, p. 203.

72. Athanasius, *Four Discourses Against the Arians* 1.6.

73. Athanasius, *Statement of Faith* 3; Athanasius, *Defence of the Nicene Definition* 14; Athanasius, *On the Opinion of Dionysius* 11; Athanasius, *Four Discourses Against the Arians* 2.18–82.

Lucian of Antioch believed that God could be known through His creatures, but Arius maintained that the Son only knows the Father as we do. God is in essence unknowable: 'The Father knows the Son, but the Son does not know the Father.'[74] To Arius, human beings cannot know God because in Christ we do not see God as He is. In reply, Athanasius complained, 'What is well written is ill understood by heretics'.[75] Epiphanius saw Arius as Origen brought back to life, but Paul of Samosata is another candidate as a possible influence on Arius. Arius differed from Origen over the eternity of the Son. Origen had taught that the Son was eternally, timelessly, generated by the Father, and yet not quite one with the Father. In his *Commentary on John*, Origen wrote: 'We consider, therefore, that there are three hypostases, the Father and the Son and the Holy Spirit; and at the same time we believe nothing to be uncreated but the Father.'[76] He discouraged prayer to the Son, but Arius, strangely enough at first sight, allowed it. Robert Gregg and Dennis Groh have claimed that Arius was motivated by an exemplarist soteriology, which means that we are saved by following Jesus as our example.[77]

There is some warrant for believing this is possible because of the way that Athanasius goes about replying to Arius. Athanasius argues that only the creator can redeem the creation, which implies that a teacher and example, however exalted, will not be sufficient. To Arius, for Christ to be capable of improvement and obedience, he had to possess a changeable nature. However, the surviving fragments that we have of Arius's writings do not allow us to draw the conclusion that Gregg and Groh have drawn, as Christopher Stead has pointed out.[78]

---

74. Athanasius, *Four Discourses Against the Arians* I.5-6.

75. Athanasius, *The Letters of Saint Athanasius Concerning the Holy Spirit* Letter 2.7 (trans. by C. R. B. Shapland [London: Epworth Press, 1951]).

76. Origen, *Commentary on John* 2.6 (ANF 10:328).

77. Robert Gregg and Dennis Groh, *Early Arianism: A View of Salvation* (Philadelphia, PA: Fortress Press, 1981), p. 97.

78. Stead, 'Arius in Modern Research,' p. 36.

In Arius's theology, God was not always Father but became the Father when He created the Son before all time. While Arius could speak in a triadic way of God, the three persons were not all alike in majesty.[79] Hence, 'there are three hypostases: Father, Son, and Holy Spirit. And God, the cause of all things, alone is without beginning, while the Son ... was given existence by the only Father.'[80] In his letter to Alexander, Arius and his supporters confessed Christ as a 'perfect creature of God, but not as one of the creatures'. This is rather a confusing notion, which in Athanasius's view was 'vomited from their heretical hearts'.[81] To Athanasius, God is 'ever Father of the Son',[82] and is never without His Word and Wisdom.[83] As he put it: 'For the Father being everlasting, His Word and His Wisdom must be everlasting.'[84] God does not acquire Fatherhood, wisdom, and speech with the addition of Christ as the Son, Wisdom, and the Word. The Father and the Son share an eternal self-sufficient community of essence.

It would be difficult to overestimate the importance of this debate and the passions that it aroused. To view Christ as God is one thing, to view Him as the highest of the angels is quite another. Athanasius may have misrepresented the complexities of the debate, as David Gwynn has charged,[85] but ultimately many who were opposed to Athanasius believed in a Christ in whom the fullness of deity did not quite dwell (cf. Col. 2:9). Rather famously, Gregory of Nyssa was later to record the situation in Constantinople:

---

79.   Socrates, *Church History* 1.26.

80.   Epiphanius, *Panarion* 69.8.1.

81.   Athanasius, *Councils of Ariminum and Seleucia* 16.

82.   Athanasius, *Defence of the Nicene Definition* 11.

83.   Ibid., 15.

84.   Athanasius, *Four Discourses Against the Arians* 1.9.

85.   Gwynn, *Eusebians*, p. 177.

> If in this city you ask a shopkeeper for change, he will argue
> with you about whether the Son is begotten or unbegotten. If
> you inquire about the quality of bread, the baker will answer,
> 'The Father is greater, the Son is less.' And if you ask the bath
> attendant to draw your bath, he will tell you that the Son was
> created ex nihilo.[86]

It is perhaps noteworthy that the three spokesmen in Gregory's
lament each come from an Arian standpoint, so popular did
some form of Arianism become in what was, after 330, the
empire's capital. Lewis Ayres is right to warn, 'No clear party
sought to preserve Arius's theology.'[87] Arian theology proved
to be a diverse creed, and Arius should not be viewed as the
founder of a theological school, but there is still a need to give a
convenient label to those groups who gave differing answers to
the New Testament confession that while Jesus is Lord, yet there
is only one God.

Alexander responded with some swiftness—R. P. C. Hanson
even says his response was 'at least precipitate'[88]—although
Sozomen rather strangely portrays him as vacillating, inclining
to one party, then the other.[89] In 318, Alexander delivered a
series of sermons on the deity of Christ. Alexander's slogan was:
'God ever, the Son ever.'[90] A provincial synod, in either 321 or
323, excommunicated two bishops, namely Secundus of Libyan
Ptolemais and Theonas of Marmarica, six presbyters (including
two with the name of Arius), and six deacons. These were
banished from Alexandria. At first, Alexander seems to have
hoped that the heresy would spend itself and not spread, but
he came to portray it as possibly 'the forerunner of Antichrist'.[91]

---

86. Cited in Hanson, *Search for the Christian Doctrine*, p. 806.

87. Ayres, *Nicaea and its Legacy*, p. 13.

88. Hanson, *Search for the Christian Doctrine*, p. 145.

89. Sozomen, *Church History* 1.15.

90. Luibhéid, *The Council of Nicaea*, p. 25.

91. Athanasius, *Deposition of Arius* 1. Also see Athanasius, *Defence Against the Arians* 90.

The authenticity of this document has been questioned, but it bears the imprint of Athanasius's simple and vigorous style.

This led to some street fighting and protests, an ominous sign of things to come. Arius appealed to Eusebius of Nicomedia whom he called 'faithful and orthodox', and signed himself off as 'a fellow-disciple of Lucian', who was, it will be recalled, one of the martyrs in Antioch during the Great Persecution.[92] Eusebius of Nicomedia took Arius's side and held another council in Bithynia, which predictably supported Arius. Thus it was that two church councils were opposed to one another – yet another ominous sign of things to come. A council in Caesarea in Palestine restored Arius, but enjoined submission to Alexander, and urged Arius to 'strive incessantly to be restored to peace and communion with him'.[93] Furthermore, as Theodoret recorded: 'The common people were witnesses of these controversies and judges of what was said on either side, and some applauded one party and some the other.'[94] Socrates too notes that 'confusion everywhere prevailed', and 'the people also divided, some siding with one party, and some with the other.'[95] Alexander replied to these developments in an encyclical letter. The controversy spread over the whole Eastern Church. Paulinus, the bishop of Tyre, was one of a number who supported Arius. According to Rubenstein, the Eusebians probably constituted a majority at this stage,[96] but this is probably a good way of misreading the evidence.

The emperor Constantine was not a man to look upon ecclesiastical disorder with equanimity. He had sought to put down Donatism in North Africa and was in no mood to stomach a theological dispute in Egypt. Constantine did not portray the

92.   Theodoret, *Church History* 1.4.

93.   Sozomen, *Church History* 1.15.

94.   Theodoret, *Church History* 1.5.

95.   Socrates, *Church History* 1.6.

96.   Rubenstein, *When Jesus Became God*, p. 61.

dispute in doctrinal terms, and it was in Eusebius of Caesarea's interest not to do so either, and so he wrote of the controversy: 'At length it reached the bishops themselves, and arrayed them in angry hostility against each other, on pretense of a jealous regard for the doctrines of divine truth.' It was a matter of 'the strife of words'.[97] Constantine wrote to both parties, Alexander and Arius,[98] but failed to stem the tide of controversy. His theological adviser, Ossius of Cordova (in Spain), was more decided in these matters; he regarded Arius as a menace.

At Antioch, early in 325, there was a council presided over by Ossius. The council declared that the Son was begotten in 'an ineffable, indescribable manner'.[99] Suspended sentences were passed on Eusebius of Caesarea, Theodotus of Laodicea, and Narcissus of Neronias. The authenticity of this synod has been contested, with some reason, but perhaps not sufficient reason, by Louis Duchesne[100] and R. V. Sellers.[101]

If the synod is authentic, Eusebius of Caesarea came to Nicaea a condemned man. This is difficult to reconcile with Sozomen's claim that Eusebius delivered the opening address at Nicaea.[102] Eusebius is not easy to categorise theologically. Rowan Williams,[103] G. C. Stead, and Timothy Barnes[104] portray the Caesarean Eusebius as an Arian supporter, but Colm Luibhéid, like Socrates before him, tries to make him sound as Nicenely orthodox as possible.[105] R. P. C. Hanson defines his

97. Eusebius, *Life of Constantine* 2.41.

98. Ibid., 2.65.

99. Ayres, *Nicaea and its Legacy*, pp. 50–51.

100. Louis Duchesne, *Early History of the Christian Church* (London: John Murray, 1922), 2:108. n.2.

101. R. V. Sellers, *Eustathius of Antioch* (Cambridge: Cambridge University Press, 1928), p. 22–23, n.2.

102. Sozomen, *Church History* 1.19.

103. Williams, *Arius*, p. 61.

104. Barnes, *Constantine and Eusebius*, p. 265.

105. Socrates, *Church History* 2.21; Luibhéid, *The Council of Nicaea*, pp. 57–59.

theology as modified Arianism.[106] Certainly, Eusebius became an implacable, yet evasive, opponent of Athanasius, who in turn regarded him as 'at first an accomplice of the Arian heresy',[107] although he later made cogent use of the fact that Eusebius had actually signed the creed at Nicaea.

D. S. Wallace-Hadrill says that Eusebius' position was 'ultimately indefensible'. Certainly, it is difficult to attach a clear meaning to Eusebius's statement that the Logos was 'not at one time non-existent and existent at another, but existent before eternal time and pre-existent and ever with the Father as His Son ... unspeakably and unthinkably to us brought into being from all time or rather before all time'.[108] He declared that 'The Son is himself God, but not *true God*.'[109] With some reason, Frances Young has called him 'an amateur when it comes to theology and philosophy.'[110]

106. Hanson, *Search for the Christian Doctrine*, p. 59.

107. Athanasius, *To the Bishops of Africa* 6.

108. D. S. Wallace Hadrill, *Eusebius of Caesarea* (London: A. R. Mowbray, 1960), p. 132.

109. Cited in Jon M. Robertson, *Christ as Mediator: A Study of the Theologies of Eusebius of Caesarea, Marcellus of Ancyra and Athanasius of Alexandria*, Oxford Theology and Religion Monographs (Oxford: Oxford University Press, 2007), p. 80.

110. Frances Young, *From Nicaea to Chalcedon* (London: SCM, 1983), p. 17.

3

'WE BELIEVE IN ONE GOD ...'

The Council of Nicaea and Its Immediate Aftermath

The Council of Nicaea (325)

In the early 320s, Licinius had banned all church councils, but Constantine, initially at least, considered that one was needed to resolve the multitude of controversies of the day. At the time of the Antiochene synod another synod was apparently already called to be held at Ancyra (where the significant figure of Marcellus was the bishop), but there was a change of venue to Nicaea (Iznik in modern Turkey), which is closer to Nicomedia, the site of the imperial palace. Constantine only mentioned that the air was good, transport available, and the facilities fine.[1] It was a time of political as well as ecclesiastical unrest, and Constantine would be close enough to take part in the proceedings. Time was at a premium, and the imperial transport and postal systems were placed at the disposal of the bishops.

The Council of Nicaea convened in May 325 in Bithynia and finished at the end of July. It is regarded as the first ecumenical or worldwide council of the church and is viewed by Mark Noll as one of the turning points in the history of Christianity.[2] That is undoubtedly true. History needs to be read forwards before

---

1.　Eusebius, *The Life of Constantine* 3.6.

2.　Mark Noll, *Turning Points* (Grand Rapids, MI: Baker Books, 1997), chapter 2.

57

it is understood backwards. At the time it was not so obvious that the creed of Nicaea would see out the decade, let alone the centuries. Indeed, Hilary of Poitiers (in Gaul) commented that he had been a bishop for some years before he ever heard of the Nicene Creed.[3]

There is some contention over the number of bishops present: the figure of 318 is found in Hilary,[4] Epiphanius,[5] Socrates,[6] Gregory of Nazianzus,[7] and the later Athanasius[8]; over 250, says Eusebius of Caesarea[9]; and '300 more or less', say Sozomen,[10] the early Athanasius,[11] and even Socrates, the latter being no stickler for mathematical exactitude. David Gwynn puts it as low as 220.[12] Hilary saw 318 as a 'sacred' number. Indeed, it had long been regarded as such, going back as far as the second-century Epistle of Barnabas. Genesis 14:14 says that Abram put 318 troops in the field to retrieve his captured nephew, Lot. Ten is signified by I, and eight by E, which give the first two letters of Jesus' name, then T signifies 300 and is also the shape of the cross.[13] Whatever the exact number, it was significant for the emperor, as he supplied all the food.[14]

As with all the early councils of the church, the vast majority of the bishops came from the East, with possibly the only ones from the West being Caecilian of Carthage and two representatives

---

3.   Hilary of Poitiers, *On the Councils* 91.

4.   Ibid., 86.

5.   Epiphanius, *Panarion* 69.11.1.

6.   Socrates, *Church History* 1.8.

7.   Gregory of Nazianzus, *Oration* 21 (NPNF2 7:14).

8.   Athanasius, *To the Bishops of Africa* 2.

9.   Eusebius, *The Life of Constantine* 3.8.

10. Sozomen, *Church History* 1.17. He says there were about 320 bishops.

11. Athanasius, *Defence of the Nicene Definition* 3.

12. David Gwynn, *Athanasius of Alexandria: Bishop, Theologian, Ascetic, Father*, Christian Theology in Context (Oxford: Oxford University Press, 2012), p. 63.

13. *Epistle of Barnabas* 9.

14. Socrates, *Church History* 1.8.

from Sylvester of Rome, as well as Ossius of Cordova who was probably chairman.[15] Philostorgius, the Arian—or to be more accurate, Eunomian—historian, makes the unreliable claim that 22 espoused the cause of Arius, but only five bishops refused to sign the creed and/or the attached anti-Arian anathemas: Eusebius of Nicomedia, Maris, Theognis of Nicaea, Theonas, and Secundus.[16] As for Athanasius, Carl Beckwith says that he did not participate in the council,[17] but as a deacon/secretary/confidant of Alexander, his role may have been more significant than Beckwith allows. Besides the 250-300 bishops at Nicaea, there were an unknown number of presbyters, deacons, acolytes, and laymen. However, it is stretching reality to say with Gwatkin, 'Athanasius had pushed the Easterners farther than they wished to go, and his victory recoiled on himself.'[18] That reads like Athanasius played a key role at the council, which is most unlikely.

Constantine was also present, having arrived, in the obsequious words of Eusebius of Caesarea, 'like some heavenly messenger of God, clothed in raiment which glittered as it were with rays of light, reflecting the glowing radiance of a purple robe, and adorned with brilliant splendor of gold and precious stones'.[19] The leading address was given by Eusebius of Caesarea (says Sozomen) or Eustathius of Antioch (says Theodoret). In view of the fact that Eusebius of Caesarea appears to have come to Nicaea under a cloud, the latter seems far more likely. The Caesarean Eusebius never claims to have given the first address, and writes simply of 'the bishop who occupied the chief place in the right division of the assembly, then rose, and, addressing the

---

15. See V. de Clercq, *Ossius of Cordova* (Washington, DC: The Catholic University of America, 1954), pp. 228-238.

16. See Philostorgius, *Church History* 1.8a (trans. Philip R. Amidon S. J. [Atlanta, GA: Society of Biblical Literature, 2007], p. 11, n,17).

17. Carl Beckwith, 'Athanasius' in *Shapers of Christian Orthodoxy*, ed. Bradley G. Green (Nottingham: Apollos, 2010), p. 155.

18. H. M. Gwatkin, *The Arian Controversy* (1908 ed. repr. Eugene, OR: Wipf and Stock, 2001), p. 39.

19. Eusebius, *Life of Constantine* 3.10.

emperor, delivered a concise speech'.[20] The bishop and historian was not one to miss opportunities to tell of his accomplishments. For example, he reprints Constantine's letters where the emperor praises him.[21]

Theodoret's claim that Eustathius of Antioch took a prominent part in the proceedings, and even delivered the opening address, is accepted by R. V. Sellers.[22] Theodoret also cites Eustathius to the effect that Eusebius put forward a blasphemous creed:

> When they began to inquire into the nature of the faith, the formulary of Eusebius was brought forward, which contained undisguised evidence of his blasphemy. The reading of it occasioned great grief to the audience, on account of its departure from the faith, while it inflicted irremediable shame on the writer.[23]

A. H. M. Jones[24] and Henry Chadwick[25] consider that this was Eusebius of Caesarea, but G. C. Stead,[26] R. P. C. Hanson,[27] and Rowan Williams[28] favor the view that it was Eusebius of Nicomedia. The latter seems rather more likely, although it needs to be remembered that Eusebius of Caesarea was to do much to alienate Eustathius of Antioch.

20. Eusebius, *Life of Constantine* 3.11.

21. Eusebius, *Life of Constantine* 3.61 and 4.30.5.

22. R. V. Sellers, *Eustathius of Antioch and His Place in the Early History of Christian Doctrine* (Cambridge: Cambridge University Press, 1928), p. 25.

23. Theodoret, *Church History* 1.7.

24. A. H. M. Jones, *Constantine and the Conversion of Europe* (1949 ed.; repr. Harmondsworth: Penguin, 1972), p. 154.

25. H. Chadwick, 'Faith and Order at the Council of Nicaea,' *Harvard Theological Review* 53, no. 3 (1960): p. 171, n.2.

26. G. C. Stead, "Eusebius" and the Council of Nicaea,' *Journal of Theological Studies* 24 (1973): p. 100.

27. R. P. C. Hanson, *The Search for the Christian Doctrine of God: The Arian Controversy* 318–381 (Edinburgh: T&T Clark, 1988), p. 161.

28. Rowan Williams, *Arius: Heresy and Tradition* (London: Darton, Longman and Todd, 1987), p. 69.

Proceedings were lively enough, but clarity was lacking. According to Socrates, 'it seemed like a contest in the dark, as neither side appeared to understand clearly the ground on which they abused the other'.[29] No contemporary record exists of the Nicene debates, and the finished creed has been preserved in the writings of Athanasius, Socrates, and Basil of Caesarea, as well as the acts of the Council of Chalcedon in 451. There was a diversity of theological views at Nicaea, and it is misleading to see Athanasians lining up against Arians. That said, the issue of the deity of Christ is a crucial one, and one of three major issues discussed at the Council. The other two were the date of Easter and the promulgation of Canon Law.

Eusebius of Caesarea seems to have produced a creed from his own church, and its wording is often thought to have provided the basis for the creed drawn up at Nicaea.[30] Eusebius's own description is worth recording:

> When this formulary was set forth by us, no one found occasion to gainsay it; but our beloved emperor was the first to testify that it was most orthodox, and that he coincided in opinion with it; and he exhorted the others to sign it, and to receive all the doctrine it contained, with the single addition of the one word—consubstantial.[31]

Eusebius was always one to recognise the theological genius of the emperor, even if others have struggled to discern this.

The Nicene Creed of 325 was not identical with what is called the Nicene Creed today. The relevant portion of the original creed is as follows:

> We believe in one God Father Almighty maker of all things, seen and unseen: And in one Lord Jesus Christ the Son of God, begotten as only begotten of the Father, that is of the substance

---

29.   Socrates, *Church History* 1.23.

30.   F. F. Bruce, *The Spreading Flame* (repr. 1976; Exeter: Paternoster, 1958), pp. 305-306.

31.   Theodoret, *Church History* 1.11.

(*ousia*) of the Father, God of God, Light of Light, true God of true God, begotten not made, consubstantial (*homoousios*) with the Father, through whom all things came into existence, both things in heaven and things on earth; who for us men and for our salvation came down and was incarnate and became man, suffered and rose again the third day, ascended into the heavens, is coming to judge the living and the dead:
And in the Holy Spirit.

To this initial creed were added the following anathemas: 'But those who say, "There was a time when he did not exist," and "Before being begotten he did not exist," and that he came into being from non-existence, or who allege that the Son of God is of another *hypostasis* or *ousia*, or is alterable or changeable, these the Catholic and Apostolic Church condemns.'

Hence the Council of Nicaea declared the full deity of the Son of God. In one sense, *homoousios* became the symbol of the whole dispute, although this did not happen immediately. In fact, *ousia* is not necessarily a technical theological term. It is only found in the Bible in Luke 15:12–13 to describe the 'stuff' or 'substance' belonging to the prodigal son. Alastair Logan suggests that Marcellus of Ancyra may have been the one to suggest *ousia* and its cognates to Alexander and Ossius.[32] This would help to explain the difficulties that the Nicene formula came to experience in a world that was becoming increasingly suspicious of Marcellus and Eustathius.

Thomas Weinandy has summarised the four charges that were often brought against *homoousios*:[33]

(a) It was not a biblical term;
(b) It had been condemned at the Council of Antioch in 268;
(c) It could be interpreted as demanding two gods;
(d) It could be viewed as Sabellian.

---

32. Alastair H. B. Logan, 'Marcellus of Ancyra and the Councils of a.d. 325: Antioch, Ancyra, and Nicaea,' *Journal of Theological Studies* 43 (October 1992): p. 442.

33. Thomas Weinandy, *Athanasius: A Theological Evaluation* (Aldershot: Ashgate, 2007), pp. 74–78. See Athanasius, *Defence of the Nicene Definition* 1 for the accusation that Nicaea should have confined itself to Scriptural terms.

Athanasius felt the force of the first argument and he sought to counter it. He argued that 'though a man use terms not in Scripture, it makes no difference so that his meaning be religious'. After all, the devil cited Scripture (Matt. 4:5-7) and Paul cited pagan writers (see Acts 17:28; 1 Cor. 15:33; Titus 1:12).[34] Regarding the condemnation of *homoousios* by the Council of Antioch in deposing Paul of Samosata, who also was the bishop of Antioch, there is much contention and little light. It is not certain what exactly Paul of Samosata taught about Christ's person. He seems to have been some kind of adoptionist, who believed that God adopted Jesus as His Son, and it is possible that he accused his opponents of being Sabellians or Monarchians who viewed the Father and the Son as one person. Hence, the council repudiated *homoousios* as understood in that bodily sense.[35] This may help to explain why the East became so suspicious of the term sixty years later.

Eusebius of Caesarea feared *homoousios* as a Sabellian term— Arius thought it was even Manichaean[36]—and says that it was only after 'mature reflection and after having subjected it to thorough examination in the presence of our most beloved emperor' that he was able to sign the Nicene formulary of faith.[37] Eusebius writes like one who was feeling a measure of anxiety and discomfort, as one who was seeking to clear his name rather than one who was solving theological issues.

Louis Duchesne was to write of Eusebius's expertise in 'clothing his ideas in a diffuse and flowing style, and in using many words to say nothing'.[38] G. L. Prestige lamented that Eusebius's 'fumbling theology afforded great encouragement to

---

34.   Athanasius, *Councils of Ariminum and Seleucia* 39.

35.   Ibid., 45. Also see Hanson, *Search for the Christian Doctrine*, p. 71.

36.   See Lewis Ayres, *Nicaea and its Legacy: An Approach to Fourth-Century Trinitarian Theology* (Oxford: Oxford University Press, 2006), p. 93.

37.   Theodoret, *Church History* 1.11.

38.   Louis Duchesne, *Early History of the Christian Church* (London: John Murray, 1922), 2:104.

the Arians'.[39] Even R. P. C. Hanson becomes frustrated with him: 'His style is elaborate and ineffective and he has little skill at expressing his thoughts clearly or preserving strict intellectual consistency.'[40] The church's first great historian was no great theologian, although he wrote more theology than history. He signed the formula with crossed fingers and then proceeded to misunderstand and misrepresent it. Rather unhelpfully, about the year 320, he had written to Alexander that the Arian party did not believe that the Son was created, but nevertheless 'he who is' has begotten 'he who is not'.[41] As R. M. Grant noted, bishops in life, as in chess, move obliquely![42]

Eusebius of Caesarea presents a rather irenic picture of the council, but it must have had its moments. Arius, Secundus, and Theonas were excommunicated and later exiled with the deacon Euzoïus. Socrates assumes that Eusebius of Nicomedia and Theognis of Nicaea were exiled, but adds that they soon returned after signing a profession of faith.[43] Sozomen thought they signed the creed but not the deposition of Arius.[44] Theodoret thought that only Secundus of Ptolemais and Theonas of Marmarica were exiled at the close of the council because they alone of the bishops refused to put their names to the creed. Meanwhile, Philostorgius says that Eusebius, Theognis, and Maris (of Chalcedon) were prepared to sign a text containing *homoiousios* and they were only exiled to Gaul three months later.[45] Athanasius implies that the condemnation of the Bithynians was distinct from that of the clerics anathematised at the council. Constantine seems

39. G. L. Prestige, *God in Patristic Thought* (London: SPCK, 1964), p. 140.

40. Hanson, *Search for the Christian Doctrine*, p. 46.

41. See Ayres, *Nicaea and its Legacy*, p. 60.

42. R. M. Grant, 'Religion and Politics at the Council of Nicaea,' *Journal of Religion* 55 (1975): p. 12.

43. Socrates, *Church History* 1.8.

44. Sozomen I.14.

45   Philostorgius, *Church History* 1.9a, 9c, 10.

to have been worried about Eusebius of Nicomedia's previous closeness to Licinius.[46]

It is puerile to depict the Arian debate as one over an iota. Constantine, followed much later by Gibbon, saw no reason why peace should not prevail. He had warned Alexander and Arius about dissension over 'this very insignificant subject of controversy'.[47] Peace was a primary virtue in Constantine's political outlook. He declared: 'I find the cause to be of a truly insignificant character, and quite unworthy of such fierce contention.'[48] Constantine would have felt keenly the fact that divisions amongst the Christians meant that Christianity was being mocked, even in the theaters.[49] He warned against disunion over 'some trifling and foolish verbal difference between ourselves' over 'points so trivial and altogether unessential'.[50] Constantine preached peace to the bishops, whether they believed in the full deity of Christ or not: 'You are in truth of one and the same judgment: you may therefore well join in communion and fellowship.'[51] Political leaders tend to dislike theological disputes.

The Council also dealt with a number of other issues, and passed what Leo Davis calls 'a collection of ad hoc measures characterized by cautious moderation'.[52] It decided on the date of Easter, with Jewish calculations revolving around the 14th day of Nisan being rejected. This solidified the practice of following a Good Friday-Easter Sunday sequence rather than observing a particular set of dates (which, of course, would mean that the days changed from year to year). Melitian and Novatianist

---

46. Williams, *Arius*, p. 72.

47. Socrates, *Church History* 1.7.

48. Eusebius, *Life of Constantine* 2.68.

49. Socrates, *Church History* 1.6.

50. Eusebius, *Life of Constantine* 2.71.

51. Ibid., 2.70.

52. Leo Donald Davis, S. J., *The First Seven Ecumenical Councils* (325-787): *Their History and Theology* (Minnesota, MN: Michael Glazier, 1990), p. 67.

baptisms and ordinations were pronounced valid, but not the baptisms or ordinations of Paul of Samosata. Melitian clergy were to submit to Alexander as the bishop of Alexandria, but Athanasius apparently considered that Nicaea was too lenient with the Melitians.[53]

The special status of the see of Alexandria was also recognised; its authority extended over Egypt, Libya, and Pentapolis. Special honor was given to the sees of Rome, Alexandria, and Antioch, whose bishops became patriarchs, and after the dedication of Constantinople in 330, it was soon added to the list. Bishops were not to move from see to see, while canon five (of the twenty passed) declared that synods would meet twice a year in every province to deal with excommunications. Eunuchs and usurers were forbidden from being ordained as clerics.

Despite his youth, Athanasius must have played some part in proceedings at Nicaea, even though that almost certainly did not include making speeches. To be somewhat anachronistic, the young and short Athanasius appeared to have triumphed over the ageing but very tall and thin Arius. The Creed, which was drawn up, was obviously designed to exclude an Arian understanding of Christ's person. Constantine then invited all the bishops to a magnificent banquet—a far cry from the days of the Great Persecution. Eusebius of Caesarea was overwhelmed: 'One might have thought that a picture of Christ's kingdom was thus shadowed forth, and a dream rather than reality.'[54] By 25 July 325, Constantine was celebrating his twentieth year as Augustus and the conclusion of the first general council of the church. He was hopeful that 'nothing might be henceforth left for discussion or controversy in matters of faith'.[55]

No doubt Athanasius was also hopeful that theological controversy might abate, but he did not share the emperor's view that it was a minor matter. That said, it is also true that

53. Athanasius, *Defence Against the Arians* 59.

54. Eusebius, *Life of Constantine* 3.15.

55. Socrates, *Church History* 1.9.

Athanasius was never one to simply fight for a word. For twenty years after the council, Athanasius barely used the term *homoousios*. What mattered to him was the truth it conveyed and not the form of words—that the Son is co-eternal with the Father. Athanasius would have been well aware that many in the East were wary of *homoousios* as a Sabellian term, whereby Christ was viewed as simply a mode of God. In Sabellianism, there is only one person in the Godhead, so Christ and the Father are seen as one person. This explains Athanasius's caution and also indicates that his understanding of the Trinity was nuanced and balanced, without any trace of fanaticism. To Athanasius, 'God is not as man, that we should dare to ask human questions about him.'[56] He knew that the finite stood before the infinite, and that 'it is better in perplexity to be silent and believe, than to disbelieve on account of the perplexity'. [57]

The next few years, however, made it clear just how fragile the Nicene victory was. Trouble erupted for Constantine within his own household. The emperor had determined to act against those guilty of serious sexual offenses. Constantine himself had discarded his wife Minervina in 307 in order to marry Fausta, by whom he had three sons: Constantine, Constantius, and Constans. Charges were brought against Minervina's son, Crispus, and he was executed. Eusebius of Caesarea had compared Constantine and Crispus to God the Father and Jesus the Saviour,[58] but what was always inappropriate, if not blasphemous, now appeared to be a highly inconvenient mockery.

Constantine's mother, Helena, then intervened by raising evidence which cast doubt on the guilt of Crispus and raised the likelihood of Fausta's culpability. Fausta was then asphyxiated in the steam baths at the imperial palace. This may have been

---

56. Athanasius, *The Letters of Saint Athanasius Concerning the Holy Spirit* 1.15, trans. C. R. B. Shapland (London: Epworth Press, 1951).

57. Athanasius, *Four Discourses Against the Arians* 2.36.

58. Eusebius, *Church History* 10.9.

murder or it may have been suicide. In the aftermath of this, Helena—at the age of eighty—made a pilgrimage to the Holy Land, supposedly to find the True Cross and heal the sick. She died on her return. Ossius, meanwhile, made his way back to Spain, perhaps disgusted by his close-up view of imperial politics. For all that, MacMullen's comment is just plain silly: 'The empire had never had on the throne a man given to such bloodthirsty violence as Constantine.'[59]

59. Ramsay MacMullen, *Christianizing the Roman Empire A.D.100–400* (New Haven, CT: Yale University Press, 1984), p. 50.

4

'BEGOTTEN OF THE FATHER WITHOUT BEGINNING AND ETERNALLY':

A Continued Post-Nicene Christological Conflict between Athanasius and the Empire

Nicaea dismantled: patriarch in troubled times (328–335)

The Nicene consensus surprisingly unraveled over the next fifty years or so, the process beginning almost immediately. There were at least twenty councils called, numerous treatises were written, creeds were composed, bishops were deposed, and church unity lost. There are probably a number of reasons, both theological and political, for this. We have already raised four theological charges that were often brought against the *homoousios*: it was not a biblical term; it had been condemned at the Council of Antioch in 268; it could be interpreted as demanding two gods; and it could be viewed as Sabellian. To these should be added some political issues:

1. The attitude of the emperor. Constantine was no theologian, and as an adherent of a minority religion, he wanted to rule an undivided empire. An undivided church would help achieve that.

2. Athanasius's friendship with a bishop like Marcellus of Ancyra no doubt contributed to the suspicion that Athanasius himself may have been theologically suspect.

3. There were doubts regarding Athanasius's moral and spiritual qualities as a bishop. Some were ready to believe that he possessed a violent and bullying streak.

At the same time, the Arians were licking their wounds in exile—Arius and Euzoïus were in Illyria, while Eusebius of Nicomedia was in Gaul, perhaps with Theognis. Eustathius of Antioch then made the tactical error of penning a critique of Eusebius of Caesarea. This provoked a counter-attack in the form of a council convened by Eusebius. To paraphrase Sozomen's summary: 'Eustathius accused Eusebius of altering the doctrines ratified by the Council of Nicaea, while the latter declares that he approved of all the Nicene doctrines, and reproached Eustathius for cleaving to the heresy of Sabellius.'[1] The other great fifth-century church historian, Socrates, tended to view Eusebius as fully orthodox, and was thus bewildered by the dispute between Eustathius and Eusebius.[2]

Even R. V. Sellers, who states that Eustathius was less Sabellian than Marcellus of Ancyra, admits that he probably understood *homoousios* in 'a Sabellianising sense'.[3] Eustathius was duly accused of Sabellianism and of immorality for good measure,[4] found guilty, and deposed. Joseph Lienhard dates this to 330, which he regards as more probable than the other possible dates, 326[5] or 331.[6] R. P. C. Hanson argues for a date of 328 or 329.[7] Timothy Barnes opts for moral delinquency and accepts that Eustathius was 'vulnerable to such accusations', which presumably means he thinks he was guilty of some sexual sin and of insulting Constantine's mother, Helena, by calling

1.   Sozomen, *Church History* 2.19.

2.   Socrates, *Church History* 1.23.

3.   R. V. Sellers, *Eustathius of Antioch and His Place in the Early History of Christian Doctrine* (Cambridge: Cambridge University Press, 1928), pp. 95, 99.

4.   Socrates, *Church History* 1.24.

5.   T. G. Elliott, 'Constantine and the Arian Reaction after Nicaea', *Journal of Ecclesiastical History* 43, no. 2 (1992): p. 179.

6.   Joseph T. Lienhard, 'Marcellus of Ancyra in Modern Research,' *Theological Studies* 43, no. 3 (1982): p. 488.

7.   R. P. C. Hanson, 'The Fate of Eustathius of Antioch,' *Zeitschrift für Kirchengeschichte* 95 (1984): pp. 171-179.

her a chambermaid.[8] However, the theological charges sound more convincing than the moral ones, although R. V. Sellers admits that Eustathius was 'a man of provocative temper'.[9] Not surprisingly, Socrates again scratches his head over the exact nature of Eustathius's deposition.[10]

The Council of Nicaea was one of the turning points in church history, but that was not immediately obvious at the time. As H. M. Gwatkin put it: 'The victory of Nicaea was rather a surprise than a solid conquest.'[11] R. P. C. Hanson has termed it 'a Pyrrhic victory'.[12] More graphically and memorably, Hilaire Belloc has commented: 'In the Council, Arianism was swamped. The numerical vote was overwhelming—but counting noses is never a final operation in human affairs.'[13]

Within a relatively short space of time, the Arian star was rising. At least six other bishops—Asclepas of Gaza, Paul of Constantinople, Euphration of Balanea, Cymatus of Paltus, Carterius of Antarados, and Eutropius of Adrianople—were to suffer the same fate as Eustathius, and later Marcellus and Athanasius. The well-known Arian, Paulinus of Tyre, replaced Eustathius as bishop of Antioch. Furthermore, Arius and Euzoïus were received in the imperial court in November 327, when their profession, which R. P. C. Hanson labels 'an entirely colourless creed,'[14] was accepted by Constantine as orthodox. Some years later, in 336, Marcellus of Ancyra joined Eustathius as an exile. Marcellus had written against Asterius from Cappadocia, whom

8.   Timothy Barnes, *Constantine and Eusebius* (Cambridge, MA: Harvard University Press, 1981), p. 227.

9.   Sellers, *Eustathius of Antioch*, p. 47.

10. Socrates, *Church History* 1.23-24.

11. H. M. Gwatkin, *Studies of Arianism* (Cambridge: Deighton Bell, 1882), p. 50.

12. R. P. C. Hanson, *The Search for the Christian Doctrine of God: The Arian Controversy 318-381* (Edinburgh: T&T Clark, 1988), p. 171.

13.. Hilaire Belloc, *The Battle Ground* (London: Cassell, 1936), p. 292.

14. Hanson, *Search for the Christian Doctrine*, p. 8.

Athanasius accused of sacrificing in the Great Persecution.[15] So extreme was Asterius that Athanasius regarded his treatise as 'on par with the crime of his sacrifice'.[16] To Asterius, the Son reveals the Father in the same way that the creation reveals the creator (Rom. 1:20).[17]

Marcellus and Eusebius of Caesarea engaged in a vigorous pamphlet war, not altogether unlike the way Eustathius and Eusebius had disputed earlier. Eusebius wrote *Against Marcellus* and *Ecclesiastical Theology* in order to refute the bishop of Ancyra. For many Easterners, Marcellus seemed more theologically dangerous than Arius. To Marcellus, God is to be understood in terms of absolute monotheism. God as Trinity only exists in economic terms, in order to bring about redemption. He rejected any use of 'person' (*hypostasis* or **prosōpon**) or 'essence' (*ousia*) in the plural and has been understood to view God as a monad who expanded into a dyad, then a triad. He viewed the Word as always united to God, but not so the Son. Appealing to 1 Corinthians 15:24–28, Marcellus maintained that God in himself is not Triune.[18] Perhaps not unreasonably, Joseph T. Lienhard portrays Marcellus as one who changed his theological views over time: 'Marcellus was, perhaps, easily swayed and a little fickle, but not obstinate in his beliefs.'[19]

Many historians have followed the researches of Otto Seeck and believed that the Council of Nicaea was reconvened in 327.[20]

---

15. Athanasius, *Councils of Ariminum and Seleucia* 18.

16. Ibid., 18.

17. Ibid., 18.

18. See Jon M. Robertson, *Christ as Mediator: A Study of the Theologies of Eusebius of Caesarea, Marcellus of Ancyra and Athanasius of Alexandria*, Oxford Theology and Religion Monographs (Oxford: Oxford University Press, 2007), pp. 98–112, 126.

19. Joseph T. Lienhard, *Contra Marcellum* (Washington, D.C.: The Catholic University of America Press, 1999), p. 156.

20. For example, Robert Archie Riall, 'Athanasius Bishop of Alexandria: The Politics of Spirituality (Egypt)' (PhD dissertation, University of Cincinnati, 1987), pp. 10–12, 19–20, 363–64; T. G. Elliott, 'Constantine and "the Arian Reaction after Nicaea",' *Journal of Ecclesiastical History* 43, no. 2 (1992): p. 183.

Hanson takes this seriously,[21] while Riall even considers that it is 'assured'. It must be admitted that it is mentioned by such fourth-century authors as Eusebius of Caesarea and Julius of Rome. No minutes were kept at Nicaea, but canon five provided for subsequent provincial councils twice a year. Because of this, Hans-Georg Opitz maintained that the so-called reconvened Nicene Council was actually only a provincial council. This should probably be identified with the Council of Nicomedia, which was summoned by Constantine to meet in early 328.[22]

Whatever the case, the Arian bishops were restored to their episcopal positions. The major sees of Antioch and Nicomedia were regained by the Arians. About a decade later, contrary to the canons of Nicaea, Eusebius of Nicomedia was promoted to become the bishop of Constantinople. No doubt the two main factors in the change in the ecclesiastical climate were Constantine's desire for peace in the church, and the Eastern suspicion of the term *homoousios*. In a startling and unpredicted reversal of fortunes, the major decisions of Nicaea had been overturned in the space of about two years.

The emperor might embrace broad-church views, but Alexander was determined that Arius was not to be readmitted to the church in Alexandria. Alexander is said by Theodoret to have died five months after the Council of Nicaea, that is, in 326,[23] but the Alexandrian bishop is usually thought to have died on 17 April 328. Athanasius was probably consecrated on 8 June 328 in keeping with the wishes of the dying Alexander.

Sozomen says that Athanasius left the city in an attempt to escape the episcopate, but Alexander's message was 'O Athanasius, you think to escape, but you will not escape.'[24] Arian authorities give a less edifying version. There were a

21.   Hanson, *Search for the Christian Doctrine*, p. 174.

22.   Cf. Williams, *Arius*, p. 74.

23.   Theodoret, *Church History* 1.25.

24.   Sozomen, *Church History* 2.17.

number of claims made at the time of Athanasius's ordination as bishop, beginning with the accusation that he was not yet thirty years of age, which was traditionally the minimum canonical age for episcopal office. Philostorgius reports one account that he forced his way into the church, locked the doors, and coerced two Egyptian bishops into ordaining him.[25] John Henry Newman cited Gregory of Nazianzus to the effect that 'the bishop of Alexandria was the bishop of the whole world',[26] but that was not quite Athanasius's experience. His troubles began when he refused to accede to Constantine's wish that all be admitted to the church who desired admittance. Constantine's request, which was really a polite threat, may have been dispatched as early as the summer of 328.

Charles Kannengiesser refers to Constantine as 'versatile,'[27] and that is an adjective that might be used of his doctrinal beliefs. The emperor's words to Athanasius were:

> Having, therefore, knowledge of my will, grant free admission to all who wish to enter into the Church. For if I learn that you have hindered or excluded any who claim to be admitted into communion with the Church, I will immediately send someone who shall depose you by my command, and shall remove you from your place.[28]

Despite this threat from the Christian emperor, Athanasius refused to grant communion to Arius, Secundus, and Theonas. To Athanasius, 'the heresy which attacks Christ has no communion with the catholic church'.[29] Arianism was dismissed

---

25. Philostorgius, *Church History* 2.11.

26. John Henry Newman, *An Essay on the Development of Christian Doctrine* (1845 ed.; repr. Harmondsworth: Penguin, 1975), p. 290.

27. Charles Kannengiesser, 'Athanasius of Aleandria v. Arius: The Alexandrian Crisis,' in *The Roots of Egyptian Christianity*, eds. B. A. Pearson and James E. Goehring (Philadelphia, PA: Fortress Press, 1992), p.205.

28. Athanasius, *Defence Against the Arians* 59; Socrates, *Church History* 1.27.

29. Athanasius, *Against the Arians* 60.1.

as 'a sort of judaical impiety',[30] 'a lately invented evil'[31] which was 'not far removed from heathenism'.[32] The scene was set for a clash. F. F. Bruce puts it dramatically: 'Athanasius stood for principle at any price; Constantine for concord at any price.'[33]

Perhaps about 328, Athanasius published a statement of faith, which stated that the Son is 'begotten of the Father without beginning and eternally'.[34] At this stage, Athanasius could point to John 14:9 ('Whoever has seen me has seen the Father'), and say that the Son is like the Father.[35] Later, he would feel obliged to qualify such an ambiguous statement. It could be taken to mean that the Son is like the Father in the sense that He is godly, or it could mean that only an infinite being is like an infinite being—the latter being the sense in which Athanasius was using the expression. Athanasius asserted the true humanity of Christ, which was taken from Mary,[36] but his emphasis was on His true deity. Hence, he wrote, with a certain inelegant majesty:

> But we do not regard God the Creator of all, the Son of God, as a creature, or thing made, or as made out of nothing, for he is truly existent from him who exists, alone existing from him who alone exists, in as much as the like glory and power was eternally and conjointly begotten of the Father.[37]

In 330, Constantinople was dedicated as the new center of the ailing empire. Also, a delegation of four Melitian bishops waited on Eusebius of Nicomedia to complain of Athanasius's alleged violence. Eusebius, who according to Ammianus Marcellinus

30. Athanasius, *To the Bishops of Egypt* 8.

31. Athanasius, *History of the Arians* 66.

32. Athanasius, *To the Bishops of Egypt* 17.

33. F. F. Bruce, *The Spreading Flame* (1958 ed.; Exeter: Paternoster, 1976), p. 309.

34. Athanasius, *Statement of Faith* 1.

35. Ibid., 1.

36. Ibid., 1.

37. Ibid., 2.

was distantly related to the imperial family,[38] agreed to help them if they recognised Arius, which they did. Athanasius saw the Melitians and Arians cooperating as Herod and Pilate had done.[39] The Melitians also charged that Athanasius was demanding linen tunics or money payments, but Constantine dismissed these charges.

In the summer of 330, Athanasius travelled through the Thebaid to appoint bishops to supplant the Melitian bishops. He went upriver through Lycopolis, Hypsele, and Tentyra. The trip seems to have been quite productive. A number of former Melitians submitted to Athanasius's authority, including Tyrannus, Ammonianus, and Plusianus. Later, such former Melitians were to write on Athanasius's behalf, and represent him at the Council of Tyre in 335.[40]

A number of recurring accusations began to appear about this time against Athanasius. He was accused of laying an impost on the people for linen tunics called *sticharia*, which the state had supplied to the church for distribution, and of sending a purse of gold to a rebel. He was also accused of ordering one of his helpers, Macarius, to break the chalice of an irregularly ordained presbyter, Ischyras, in a small village called Mareotis, south-west of Alexandria.[41] There is some confusion about chronology, but there was a further charge that Athanasius had murdered and dismembered a man called Arsenius. It was an age of sorcery and magic, and Arsenius's body was supposed to have been cut up and represented by a severed hand in a wooden box. Athanasius claimed that there were 'feigned lamentations

38. Ammianus Marcellinus, *The Later Roman Empire* (A.D.354–378), trans. by Walter Hamilton (London: Penguin, 2004), 22.9 (p. 242).

39. Athanasius, *To the Bishops of Egypt* 22. See Luke 23:12.

40. See Riall, 'Athanasius Bishop of Alexandria,' p. 42; D. Wade-Hampton Arnold, *The Early Episcopal Career of Athanasius of Alexandria* (Notre Dame, IN: University of Notre Dame Press, 1991), pp. 62, 146.

41. Athanasius, *Defence Against the Arians* 60.

and fictitious tears' at Arsenius's reported death.[42] To add to the intrigue, the severed hand was supposed to have been used for sorcery and witchcraft. As Athanasius said, 'We are indeed ashamed to make any defence against such charges.'[43] He further denied any violence against anybody, saying that 'slaughter and imprisonment are foreign to our Church'.[44]

It may have been in 331 that Athanasius was summoned to Nicomedia to meet with Constantine to answer a number of charges. Athanasius attended, and the emperor was impressed by Athanasius as 'truly a man of God'. Athanasius was able to defend himself against the charge of sacrilege by claiming that Ischyras was not a real presbyter, not even a Melitian one. He maintained that the cup was not broken in a church nor on the Lord's Day.[45] This may imply that the chalice was actually broken by Macarius. To Athanasius, it was all rather disproportionate, and he asked: 'Whence comes this religious regard for the cup among those who support impiety towards Christ?'[46]

Falling ill, Athanasius remained in Nicomedia for some months before returning to Alexandria. Sometime before Easter 332, Athanasius received a new summons to appear in Antioch before Dalmatius (Constantine's half-brother) for the murder of Arsenius, the Arian bishop of Hypsele. John Arcaph—the Melitian bishop of Memphis, who had replaced the now-deceased Melitius as leader of the schismatics—had made the charge. Arcaph appears to have been more hostile to Athanasius than was his predecessor, possibly because of Athanasius's success in winning over former Melitians. The case against Athanasius collapsed as Arsenius was found to have been hiding in a Melitian monastery in the Lower Thebes and then discovered by Athanasius's men in Tyre where he was protected

42. Ibid., 38.
43. Ibid., 5.
44. Ibid., 5.
45. Ibid., 11.
46. Ibid., 17.

by the bishop, Paulinus, and where he had been living under a false name.[47] Arsenius was, in Tillemont's words, 'convicted of being himself.'[48]

Later, it seems that Arsenius was reconciled to Athanasius,[49] which may indicate Athanasius's astuteness or generosity of spirit or both. The Melitians were embarrassed, and Constantine wrote to Athanasius to pledge his imperial support.[50] Strengthened by this, Athanasius toured the Libyan Pentapolis in 332. Early in 334, he went on a tour of the Delta. These may have been routine pastoral visits or they may have been attempts to bring peace to trouble spots. Whatever the case, from between 330-334 Athanasius undertook three visits to desert regions—which may have stood him in good stead during his third, fourth and fifth exiles when he sought refuge in the desert

Late in 332 or in 333 Arius had written to Constantine, asking for restoration to Alexandria or for an independent Libyan see. Arius had made the mistake of emphasising his numerical support, which the emperor took to be an implied threat. The response was hostile and belittling, and revealed Constantine's capacity for small-minded sarcasm, as he berated Arius as an *Ares* (god of war), a heretic, and a man of wasted and ascetic appearance. Arius's works were to suffer the same fate as those of Porphyry—burning. In fact, anyone not surrendering copies of Arius's works was to be executed. In T. G. Elliott's summary: 'Six pages of abuse, ridicule, scorn and vituperation end with the order to come to court to be healed.'[51] For all that, Athanasius's position was not as secure as it seemed. Constantine was a passionate and unstable man, easily moved to anger or to affection. He tended to be the friend of the last person who spoke smooth words to him.

47.　Ibid., 65.

48.　Cited in Arnold, *Early Episcopal Career of Athanasius*, p. 137.

49.　Athanasius, *Defence Against the Arians* 27.

50.　Ibid., 68.

51.　Elliott, 'Constantine,' p. 189.

The Disfavor of the First Christian Emperor: First Exile at Trier (335–337)

Constantine summoned Athanasius to a council at Caesarea in Palestine in 333 or 334, but the bishop refused to come.[52] Finally, at Tyre in July 335, sixty Eastern bishops met with forty-eight Egyptian bishops who came with Athanasius, who had been threatened if he did not attend. Socrates actually gives the impression that there were sixty bishops present altogether,[53] but he must have excluded the episcopal entourage that Athanasius brought with him. It is instructive that many ex-Melitians went with Athanasius to Tyre, and that Alexander of Thessalonica sided with Athanasius. Constantine was especially keen that the Macarius-Ischyras affair be sorted out. Some of the Arians and Melitians, who demonstrably were less than scrupulous with the truth, were willing to play on the emperor's fears.

Athanasius refuted charges of immorality and, according to Rufinus's dramatic account, produced Arsenius with both of his hands. When Arsenius's condition was revealed, by turning back one side of his cloak, then the other, Athanasius was able to indulge in his gift for sarcasm: 'Arsenius, as you see, is found to have two hands: let my accusers show the place whence the third was cut off.'[54]

Modern historians take these charges against Athanasius more seriously than the evidence warrants. R. P. C. Hanson, for example, says that the general charge of strong-arm tactics was 'abundantly justified'.[55] H. Idris Bell too says that the charges were 'not baseless' and that 'after each frustrated offensive of his enemies Athanasius allowed himself the luxury of reprisals'.[56] Athanasius never saw Arianism as a viable expression of the

---

52. Athanasius, *Defence Against the Arians* 77.

53. Socrates, *Church History* 1.20.

54. Ibid., 1.29.

55. Hanson, *Search for the Christian Doctrine*, p. 255.

56. H. Idris Bell, *Jews and Christians in Egypt* (1924 ed.; repr. Westport, CT: Greenwood Press, 1972), p. 47.

Christian faith, but he did not regard Arians as simply enemies to be confronted. On the contrary, he reminded his people that God is able to open the eyes of the Arians.[57] He urged his flock: 'Let your love overcome the malice of the heretics'.[58] The Council of Tyre appointed a commission of six Arians to investigate these charges: Theognis of Nicaea, Maris of Chalcedon, Theodorus of Thracian Heraclea, Macedonius of Mopsuestia, Ursacius of Singidunum (now called Belgrade), and Valens of Mursa. According to Athanasius, the latter two, Ursacius and Valens, had been instructed in their youth by Arius.[59] The anti-Athanasian make-up of the commission was obvious enough. Its task was to go to the village in Mareotis, where Macarius was alleged to have outraged Ischyras's church. Accompanying the Arian commission was Philagrius, who was the Prefect of Egypt and a pagan.

The council then adjourned to Jerusalem to dedicate the church of the Holy Sepulchre in September 335. At Jerusalem, the bishops also restored Arius and his followers to communion. The council at Jerusalem wrote to the church at Alexandria in an imploring and pious tone: 'We should with simple and peaceable minds receive Arius and his fellows, whom envy, that enemy of all goodness, has caused for a season to be excluded from the Church'.[60] For some time, Arius had been blurring his earlier statements that Jesus was created from nothing, that He did not know the Father, and that He was mutable and capable of sinning. Indeed, it may be more accurate to refer to Athanasius's opponents as the Eusebians rather than the Arians. Athanasius himself could refer to 'the party of Eusebius'.[61] All this was ominous for Athanasius, for Constantine was one who was wary of doctrinal controversies and had respect for the sanctity of episcopal conciliar decisions.

57. Athanasius, *On Luke 10.22* (Matt. 11.27).

58. Athanasius, *Letter 47*.

59. Athanasius, *To the Bishops of Egypt 7*.

60. Athanasius, *Defence Against the Arians 84*.

61. Athanasius, *Easter Letter 11.12*.

The bishops subsequently returned to Tyre and deposed Athanasius, who is supposed to have floated out of Tyre on a raft in the darkness. Despairing of justice, Athanasius fled to Constantinople to gain the emperor's ear. He achieved this on 30 October 335 when, dressed in rags, he stood in the middle of the road as the emperor rode into Constantinople on horseback. It must have been an emotional and dramatic moment. The emperor did not recognise the dishevelled bishop at first but then took pity on him. Little more than a week later, all had changed again.

Arriving back at the imperial palace, the bishops were disappointed to find that Constantine had annulled their decisions, so Eusebius of Nicomedia accused Athanasius of hindering the sailing of corn-vessels from Alexandria.[62] This was a serious charge, for without Egyptian grain, there would be riots throughout the empire. Some years before this, a Syrian philosopher, Sopater, had fallen foul of Constantine and been beheaded for binding the south wind by the power of magic.[63] Athanasius lost his temper, and, in Epiphanius's description, spoke painful words to the empire's first Christian emperor. The bishop warned him: 'God will judge between you and me, just as surely as you are in agreement with the traducers of my poor self.'[64] The charges of violence and contumacy seemed believable to those who wanted to believe them. R. P. C. Hanson regards Athanasius as one who was guilty of serious misconduct,[65] while even the scholarly and cautious Henry Chadwick thinks that Athanasius was guilty of violence and of threatening a dock-strike to cut off the supply of grain from Egypt to Constantinople.[66]

---

62. Athanasius, *Defence Against the Arians* 87.

63. Edward Gibbon, *The History of the Decline and Fall of the Roman Empire*, ed. by David Womersley (1776 and 1781 ed.; repr. London: Penguin, 1995), 1:800, n.108.

64. Epiphanius, Frank Williams (trans.), *The Panarion of Epiphanius of Salamis, Books II and III. De Fide*, Leiden: Brill, 2013, p. 331.

65. Hanson, *Search for the Christian Doctrine*, p. 273.

66. Henry Chadwick, *The Church in Ancient Society* (Oxford: Oxford University Press, 2003), p. 202.

Constantine erupted and replied by exiling Athanasius to Trier (or Treves) in Gaul, to the court of Constantine's son, the man who was to become Constantine II. The Melitian leader, Arcaph, was also banished. At Trier Athanasius was not unduly restricted. In 336 and 337, he sent paschal calculations to the Egyptian presbyters to communicate to the Egyptian churches. It was, said Edward Gibbon, 'a jealous ostracism, rather than ... an ignominious exile'.[67]

Exile in the imperial court at Trier was no doubt rather more comfortable than some of the other exiles that Athanasius was to experience. By mid-June of 337, soon after Constantine's death, he had left Trier. Eventually, Athanasius was able to make his way back to Alexandria in November of 337. According to Timothy Barnes, Athanasius was able to maintain his position in Alexandria by 'the systematic use of violence and intimidation',[68] which seems a remarkable achievement for one so often in exile. In reality, the support for Athanasius was spontaneous rather than engineered.

This first exile had lasted for two and a half years, but Athanasius was supported by Maximin, the bishop of Trier. Constantine died on 22 May 337, after receiving baptism from the Arian Eusebius of Nicomedia. The Eastern Church came to regard the first Christian emperor as a saint. Arius also died, about a year before the emperor. He had died suddenly, on the Sabbath (Saturday), the day before his proposed restoration—'split into pieces in the public lavatory' in Athanasius's graphic but still elusive description. Arius was thus deprived of life and communion together, dying a death reminiscent of Judas himself (Acts 1:18).[69] Epiphanius is as blunt as only he could be: 'During the night Arius went to the toilet to answer the call of nature, and burst, as Judas once did. And thus he met his

---

67. Gibbon, *History of the Decline and Fall*, 1:800–801.

68. T. D. Barnes, *Athanasius and Constantius* (Cambridge, MA: Harvard University Press, 1993), p. 32.

69. Theodoret, *Church History* 1.13; Athanasius, *To the Bishops of Egypt* 18–19.

end in a stench-filled, unclean place.'[70] Revealing the modern churchman's distaste for any notion of divine intervention in human affairs, especially to carry out judgment, Rowan Williams adopts a mocking tone: 'The emperor and the city were duly shocked and edified.'[71]

Twenty years later, Athanasius referred in rather more sensitive terms to Arius's sudden death: 'we ought not to insult the dead, though he be an enemy, for it is uncertain whether the same event may not happen to ourselves before evening'.[72] Athanasius was not at Constantinople when Arius died, and relied on a report from a presbyter, Macarius.[73] In fact, Athanasius states that he hesitated to write about the death of Arius 'lest anyone should suppose that I was exulting in the death of that man'.[74]

In the meantime, Constantine's three sons—Constantine II, Constantius, and Constans—took over the ruling of the empire. Constantine II in Trier took a kind of precedence over Constantius in Antioch and Constans in Milan. As the lead emperor, Constantine II restored all exiled bishops and the other two brothers concurred. When Athanasius returned to Alexandria, he did so without any reversal of the synodical decision to depose him at Tyre. Yet he was so popular that he could adopt the Western practice of observing Lent for forty days instead of six and having this change accepted by Egyptian Christians.[75]

It was politically imperative that Athanasius meet with Constantius II, the emperor of the East. Athanasius had made his way home via the Danubian provinces, Asia Minor, Syria,

---

70.   Epiphanius, *Panarion* 68.6.9; also 69.10.3.

71.   Williams, *Arius*, 81.

72.   Athanasius, *To the Bishops of Egypt* 19.

73.   Athanasius, *Epistle* 54.2.

74.   Ibid., *54.3*.

75.   Ibid., *6.13*. Also see Nicholas V. Russo, 'The Early History of Lent' in *Christian Reflection* (Waco, TX: The Center for Christian Ethics at Baylor University, 2013), pp. 18-19.

Lebanon, and Palestine. He seems to have met Constantius in Viminacium in Moesia in August 337, and also in Syrian Antioch. It was clear that there would be more troubles ahead. Constantius sent Paul of Constantinople into exile, and replaced him with Eusebius of Nicomedia, thus contravening the canons of Nicaea, which forbade bishops to transfer from one see to another. Paul was finally strangled in Cappadocia about 350, while Athanasius was to refer to Eusebius of Nicomedia as a man 'with an evil eye'.[76]

---

76. Athanasius, *History of the Arians* 7.

5

'FOR HIS MERCY ENDURES FOREVER'

Athanasius's Exiles, the Beginning of the Demise of Arianism, and the Final Years of Athanasius's Life

From Constantine's Death to the End of the Second Exile in Rome (337–346)

On 23 November 337, when Athanasius arrived back in Alexandria, he did so to great acclamation. It is a recurring motif in the life of Athanasius that he retained his popularity amongst the Christians of Egypt. This is difficult to explain if Athanasius was the bully and tyrant that so many modern scholars portray him to have been. Athanasius warned: 'But let a man, wherever he is, strive earnestly; for the crown is given not according to position, but according to action.'[1] Presumably, he made some attempt to follow his own exhortations.

Constantius, under the influence of Eusebius (once of Nicomedia, now of Constantinople), accused Athanasius of unauthorised resumption of his ministry, bloodshed against certain Egyptian clergy, and of appropriating corn meant for charitable purposes. Epiphanius portrays Constantius in the following terms:

> Religious and good in many ways, but in this one respect he slipped, in that he did not walk in his father's faith. The fault was not his but belongs to those who will give an account on the

---

1.   Athanasius, *Epistle* 49.9.

Day of Judgment, those who, though called bishops because of
what they appear to be, have corrupted the true faith of God.[2]

It was an unusually diplomatic portrayal by the old heresy hunter.

Another Council at Antioch, with 97 bishops in attendance,
in 338-339 saw no reason to revise the decisions of Tyre, and
so deposed Athanasius, and sent Gregory the Cappadocian
to replace him as the patriarch of Alexandria. As soon as
Constantine was dead, the Libyan, Secundus of Ptolemais,
had apparently consecrated the Arian Pistus as the bishop of
Alexandria but he quickly (and strangely) drops out of the
picture. Socrates also mentions that the Council of Antioch
appointed Eusebius of Emesa as Athanasius's replacement,
but this Eusebius refused to take up the task because of the
popularity of Athanasius.[3] This is another indication that
Athanasius was genuinely popular with his flock. The prefect of
Egypt, Philagrius, and Bishop Gregory—a pagan and an Arian,
and both Cappadocians—combined to persecute the orthodox.
In addition, Arius may have been readmitted, posthumously, to
communion.

Athanasius's defence came in the form of a council of 80
bishops which met at Alexandria in April 338 and exonerated
their bishop of all charges. It seems to be about this time that
Antony visited Alexandria to support Nicene orthodoxy. He did
fall asleep during one of Athanasius's sermons but claimed it
was 'because of the sweetness of his words'.[4] Athanasius regarded
Antony as one, who though illiterate, was 'a ready-witted and
sagacious man'.[5] Antony had a vision of mules plundering the
Church, which was understood to be a reference to the damage

2. Epiphanius, *Panarion* 69.12.5-6.

3. Socrates, *Church History* 2.9-10.

4. Robert Archie Riall, 'Athanasius Bishop of Alexandria: The Politics of Spirituality
    (Egypt)' (PhD dissertation, University of Cincinnati, 1987), p. 110. n.33.

5. Athanasius, *The Life of Antony* 72.

that the Arians would do.[6] Also, at this time Didymus the Blind may have been appointed as head of the prestigious Alexandrian catechetical school.

With the Councils of Antioch and Alexandria at loggerheads, emissaries from both were sent to Rome to enlist the support of the most influential bishopric in the West. Meanwhile, in Alexandria, Philagrius as the prefect of Egypt was hostile to Athanasius and proclaimed that Gregory was coming to replace Athanasius. Full of official pomp, Gregory arrived in Alexandria on 26 March 339. Orthodox churches were forcibly taken over, often with considerable difficulty. Athanasius contended: 'Our sufferings have been dreadful beyond endurance.'[7] Somewhat oddly, he cited the situation in Judges 19 and claimed:

> For, the treatment we have undergone surpasses the bitterness of any persecution; and the calamity of the Levite was but small, when compared with the enormities which have now been committed against the Church; or rather such deeds as these were never before heard of in the whole world, or the like experienced by anyone.[8]

The oddness of the reference, for the Levite is no spiritual giant, is undoubtedly explained by Athanasius's comment that Philagrius had long been a persecutor of the church and her virgins.[9]

According to Athanasius, disorderly characters attacked the church and Athanasius's own church building was set on fire. Virgins were assaulted, and birds and pinecones were offered on the communion table in a mockery of the Lord's Supper. Scriptures were burnt—a reminder that the Great Persecution was not far back in history—and church supplies were plundered. On Good Friday some thirty-four Christians were scourged and

---

6.   Ibid., 82.

7.   Athanasius, *Encyclical Epistle to Bishops Throughout the World* 1.

8.   Ibid., 1.

9.   Ibid., 3.

imprisoned.[10] Athanasius's own aunt perished in the persecution and he claimed that Gregory denied her a burial.[11]

The populace responded by rioting. Under threat of arrest, Athanasius sailed for Rome in Easter of 339 where he was to spend three years. Gregory also sent an emissary with a formal list of charges against Athanasius. Athanasius maintained that Gregory's secretary, Ammon, was one whom Athanasius had formerly excommunicated for his many misdeeds and impiety.[12] Not unreasonably, Julius, the bishop of Rome, proposed a council to review the matter, but he himself supported Athanasius. The beginnings of the East-West schism can be detected. The Antiochene bishops refused to participate in the review council in Rome and each side took offence at the other. In Julius's view, 'all bishops have the same and equal authority',[13] and it was not right for the Council of Tyre to undo the work of the Council of Nicaea.

The issues were becoming clouded. To many Easterners, Athanasius's condemnation at Tyre was not a doctrinal matter but moral—he was guilty of misdemeanours. To many Westerners, the issue was doctrinal—the deity of Christ was being attacked. Indeed, the issues became even cloudier. At Rome, Athanasius met another exile, Marcellus of Ancyra, whom the East regarded as Sabellian in his view of God. He was thought to teach that the Father, Son, and Holy Spirit were not three Persons but one, rather like a man who acts as a pastor, a husband, and a father. In the end, for Marcellus, there are only three roles or perhaps modes. According to Epiphanius, when he was asked for his opinion of Marcellus's doctrine, Athanasius 'neither defended him nor showed dislike for him, but only suggested with a smile that he had come close to depravity, but

---

10. Ibid., 3–4.

11. Athanasius, *History of the Arians* 13.

12. Athanasius, *Encyclical Epistle to Bishops Throughout the World* 7.

13. Athanasius, *Defence Against the Arians* 25. This is interesting in the light of subsequent Roman claims to supremacy over other bishops.

that he considered that he had cleared himself'.[14] The smile may only have indicated Athanasius's caution and wisdom gained through hard experience. In Alastair Logan's words: 'Certainly, Marcellus almost became a kind of non-person, as if one were to write the history of the Russian revolution without any mention of the part played in it by Trotsky.'[15] To Athanasius, he came to be perceived as something of a liability. The fourth of Athanasius's *Four Discourses Against the Arians*, translated in the *Nicene and Post-Nicene Fathers of the Christian Church*, includes an extended critique of Marcellus as one whose doctrine leads to Sabellianism, but the discourse is not generally regarded as authentic.[16] In any case, Jon Robertson sees little evidence that Athanasius and Marcellus had any influence on each other.[17] Sara Parvis portrays a generous Marcellus who allowed himself to be sacrificed, as it were, in order that Athanasius would be freed up to save the wider cause.[18]

When the review council met in Rome in 340, it gave Athanasius a vote of confidence. Yet all was not to go smoothly. Julius, the bishop of Rome, also supported Marcellus, something that Marcellus was not to receive from later theologians such as Basil of Caesarea, Epiphanius, and John Chrysostom.[19] Julius wanted a revision of both the synod of Tyre, which had condemned Athanasius in 335 and the synod of Constantinople, which had condemned Marcellus in 336. Western support for

---

14. Epiphanius, *Panarion* 72.4.4.

15. Alastair H. B. Logan, 'Marcellus of Ancyra and the Councils of a.d. 325: Antioch, Ancyra, and Nicaea,' *Journal of Theological Studies* 43 (1992): p. 439.

16. See Joseph T. Lienhard, 'From Gwatkin Onwards: A Guide through a Century and a Quarter of Studies on Arianism,' *Augustinian Studies* 44, no. 2 (2013): p. 277.

17. Jon M. Robertson, *Christ as Mediator: A Study of the Theologies of Eusebius of Caesarea, Marcellus of Ancyra and Athanasius of Alexandria*, Oxford Theology and Religion Monographs (Oxford: Oxford University Press, 2007), pp. 166–167.

18. Sara Parvis, *Marcllus of Ancyra and the Lost Years of the Arian Controversy, 325–345*, Oxford Early Christian Studies (Oxford: Oxford University Press, 2006), pp. 249-252.

19. Athanasius, *Defence Against the Arians* 32 (NPNF2 5:116, n.5).

Athanasius and Marcellus was viewed as interference in Eastern matters and can only have further convinced the Easterners that the Nicene Creed was defective in that one whom they regarded as Sabellian could agree to it. Eastern suspicion of *homoousios* may have been increased if, as is not unlikely, the Westerner, Ossius of Cordova, was a key figure behind the Nicene Creed.

In 340, Constantine II died while invading the dominions of his brother Constans, and Athanasius was left with no imperial protector. It was alleged that Athanasius may have advised this invasion and Timothy Barnes considers it plausible, although Rubenstein more sensibly refuses to agree with him.[20] At this stage, Athanasius was officially barred from pastoral contact with Egypt, but he wrote to his friend, Serapion, the bishop of Thmuis, and to other Egyptian and Palestinian bishops, as well as to monks. He sought to keep the perspective of eternity in the forefront of his mind, for 'all present matters are trifling compared with those which are future'.[21]

The so-called 'dedication' creed was drawn up by about ninety bishops, who met at Antioch in 341 to dedicate the 'Golden Church' of Constantine. It was not exactly Arian. In fact, the bishops maintained that as bishops they could not possibly follow Arius who was only a presbyter.[22] It was certainly intended to be anti-Sabellian or anti-Marcellan.[23] Yet those at this council did not commit themselves to the *homoousios* or to the eternity of the Son. After Easter 341, Athanasius in Rome received a letter summoning him to Milan to meet with Constans, who was only 18 years old at the time. Episcopal emissaries from Antioch wanted to consider creedal formulations. Constans

20. T. D. Barnes, *Athanasius and Constantius* (Cambridge, MA: Harvard University Press, 1993), 52; Rubenstein, *When Jesus Became God*, p. 250, n.150.

21. Athanasius, *Easter Letter* 13.4.

22. Athanasius, *On the Synods* 1.22.

23. Cf. Lewis Ayres, *Nicaea and its Legacy: An Approach to Fourth-Century Trinitarian Theology* (Oxford: Oxford University Press, 2006), pp. 118-119; R. P. C. Hanson, *The Search for the Christian Doctrine of God: The Arian Controversy 318-381* (Edinburgh: T&T Clark, 1988), pp. 123, 286-288.

then summoned Athanasius from Milan to Trier in September 342 before a council was to meet in Sardica. So far as can be known, Constans's intentions appear to have been to support Athanasius. Both Constans and Constantius II agreed that a full synod needed to be held.

Socrates says that a council met at Serdica (or Sardica, which is modern Sofia) in Illyricum in 347, but modern scholars tend to agree with Athanasius that it occurred about four or five years earlier.[24] There may have been something like 170 bishops, with a few more Westerners than Easterners at the council[25]—some elderly bishops actually died on the way—but little unity between the bishops. In many ways, the synod was a non-event as the council never met as a single body. With the exception of the Egyptians, the Eastern bishops objected to the full participation of Athanasius, and to the inclusion of the other refugee bishops, Marcellus of Ancyra, his disciple Photinus of Sirmium, as well as Asclepas of Gaza and Paul of Constantinople. They anathematised them and those who received them, including Julius of Rome and Ossius of Cordova, who was president of the council.

The Easterners asked for capital punishment if Athanasius were found in Alexandria again.[26] The Westerners, some of whom came from Greek-speaking regions, replied by excommunicating the leading Eastern bishops, declaring George's ordination void,[27] and exonerating Athanasius and Marcellus, as well as Asclepas of Gaza, as 'our dearly beloved brethren and fellow-ministers'.[28] Two Eastern bishops, Asterius

24.   Henry Chadwick, *The Church in Ancient Society* (Oxford: Oxford University Press, 2003), p. 241, n.1.

25.   See Hamilton Hess, *The Early Development of Canon Law and the Council of Serdica* (Oxford: Oxford University Press, 2002), p. 102. See also Athanasius, *History of the Arians* 15.

26.   Athanasius, *History of the Arians* 19.

27.   Ibid., 17.

28.   Athanasius, *Defence Against the Arians* 44.

from Arabia and Arius from Palestine, swapped sides and joined the Westerners. The Eusebians were accused of relying 'more upon violence than upon a judicial enquiry'.[29] On the other hand, the Western confession at Serdica is often viewed as Sabellian.[30] If the Easterners can be rightly accused of injustice, the Westerners must be said to have lacked a certain wisdom in the way they conducted themselves. Both sides assumed what they were supposed to prove.

Not surprisingly, the council, assuming it could be called a council, broke down. The Eastern bishops refused to meet with the Western Synod, and so, said Athanasius, 'their flight only confirmed the proof of their own calumnies'.[31] Henry Chadwick, however, regards the West as coercive, and says: 'Rome had dictated a verdict in advance.'[32] Episcopal territorialism was an issue and the Eastern bishops complained: 'They have thought to introduce a new law; that Eastern bishops should be judged by Western.'[33] Whichever side deserves most blame, it must be said that, to cite Chadwick, as a council, Serdica was 'spectacularly unsuccessful',[34] indeed, 'a disaster', in Lewis Ayres's view.[35]

Stephen of Antioch even hired a prostitute to try to besmirch the name of the Western delegation, notably that of Euphrates of Agrippina (Upper Gaul) but he was found out and excommunicated.[36] It was yet another indication that many in the Arian or Eusebian party were prepared to employ whatever tactics they could to gain the upper hand. On the other hand, the fact that the Western bishops had treated Athanasius, Marcellus, and Photinus as though they belonged together was

29. Athanasius, *Defence Against the Arians* 37.

30. See Hanson, *Search for the Christian Doctrine*, p. 304.

31. Athanasius, *Defence Against the Arians* 47.

32. Chadwick, *Church in Ancient Society*, p. 244.

33. Cited in Hess, *Early Development of Canon Law*, p. 100, n.10.

34. Chadwick, *Church in Ancient Society*, p. 250.

35. Ayres, *Nicaea and its Legacy*, p. 123.

36. Athanasius, *History of the Arians* 20; Sozomen, *Church History* 3.20.

problematical to the Easterners and with considerable reason. Speaking in very general terms, it seemed that to the Westerners, the East was soft on Arianism, while to the Easterners, the West was soft on Sabellianism. The rift between East and West was widening. Western support of Athanasius at Serdica meant little in immediate terms, as he was still not restored to his see.

Athanasius retired to Dacian Naissus in the Balkans, where Constantine had hailed from, in the hope that Constans would enforce the results of the council or the Western component of it. In the East, Paul failed to regain Constantinople in 342. In fact, when Constantius heard that Paul had returned to Constantinople, he dispatched his general, Hermogenes, to arrest Paul. The general, however, was killed by the mob, so Constantius himself had to arrive, and send Paul into exile to Trier. This did not augur well for Athanasius, who in any case was forced to wait out 343 while Constans was away in Britain.

About February 345, Gregory died after a long illness and Constantius, busy on the Persian front, asked Athanasius to return to Alexandria. In 344, Constans had threatened his brother with war if Athanasius and Paul (of Constantinople) were not restored to their sees.[37] Battling the Persians, Constantius had little option but to agree. However, this later embarrassed Athanasius, who was seen as one who belonged to the West. Tensions were high. Athanasius tells of ten Christians at Adrianople who were beheaded, while others elsewhere were threatened with a similar fate for rejecting Eusebianism or for supporting Athanasius's group: 'Thus this new Jewish heresy does not only deny the Lord but has also learnt to commit murder.'[38] Indeed, in Athanasius's perspective, Arianism was a form of Jewish paganism. Were it not for their servility to Constantius, Athanasius, adopting his most strident mocking

---

37.   Hanson does question this. Hanson, *Search for the Christian Doctrine*, pp. 307-308.

38.   Athanasius, *History of the Arians* 18-19.

tone, claimed that the Ariomaniacs (Arian maniacs) would have been circumcised![39]

The so-called 'Macrostich' ('long-lined') creed sent to Milan in 345 confessed the Son as 'like in all things to the Father'. Photinus of Sirmium was identified as almost adoptionist[40] (one who believed that Jesus became the Son of God by being promoted into the Godhead), and since he was a disciple of Marcellus of Ancyra, this naturally led to more suspicion being cast on him. The Easterners were required to condemn Arius before their creed was discussed. This wounded some Eastern pride and their delegates returned home.

Athanasius had gone west to Aquileia, wanting guarantees from Constantius, who insisted on freedom for the Arians in Alexandria. Only after three letters from Constantius did the wary Athanasius formally accept restoration in Alexandria. Indeed, it took a fourth letter before Athanasius's episcopal restoration was made explicit. Constantius told Athanasius that 'our fixed determination is that you should continue, agreeably to our desire, to perform the office of a Bishop in your own place'.[41] Athanasius also wanted freedom for those loyal to Eustathius in Antioch.

Athanasius went on to Jerusalem and, finally, returned home probably on 21 October 346, when he was received with great acclamation. When an emperor was coming to a city, he was usually met ten miles from its precincts, but Athanasius was met by his supporters when he was still a hundred miles from Alexandria.[42] Christopher Haas does not want to exaggerate the significance of this[43] but it was significant enough. The sailors

39.　Athanasius, *Four Discourses Against the Arians* 3.28.

40.　Cf. Epiphanius, *Panarion* 71.

41.　Athanasius, *History of the Arians* 24.

42.　Athanasius, *Introduction to Easter Letter* 17 (NPNF2 4:504). Also see: W. H. C. Frend, *The Rise of Christianity* (London: Darton, Longman and Todd, 1984), p. 532.

43.　Christopher Haas, *Alexandria in Late Antiquity* (London: The Johns Hopkins

and dockworkers of the city's twin harbors, together with many others, were glad to see their bishop return hale and hearty. Julius told the church of Alexandria: 'He returns to you now more illustrious than when he went away from you'.[44] However, this reinstatement had come about through a reluctant concession of a fearful emperor, Constantius, not a change of heart and mind on the part of an Eastern synod. The verdict of Tyre in 335 still stood.

High Hopes: 'The Golden Decade' (346–356)

On his return to Alexandria, Athanasius found that one of his loyal bishops had been exiled and another one had been put to death. A council of 94 bishops met in Alexandria in May 347. Four of the new appointees were former schismatics: Arsenius, Isaac, Isidorus, and Paulus.[45] This is yet another indication of Athanasius's capacity to absorb former opponents into his camp, which hardly fits the hostile view that Athanasius was a rigidly dogmatic megalomaniac.

For all the trials that he was still facing, life seemed to be looking more promising for Athanasius, and W. H. C. Frend, along with others, portrays this as his 'golden decade'.[46] Just before his death in 346, the Roman Consul, Petronius, sent two monks to welcome Athanasius. In addition, the influential Pachomius, the leader of the communal brand of monasticism, also close to death, gave his support to Athanasius.[47] Ursacius of Singidunum and Valens of Mursa recanted and confessed that all the charges, which had been aired against Athanasius

University Press, 1997), p. 85.

44. Athanasius, *Defence Against the Arians* 52.

45. Athanasius, *Easter Letter* 19.13.

46. Frend, *Rise of Christianity*, p. 532. Also see: Archibald Robertson, 'Prolegomena' (NPNF2 4:xlviii).

47. David Brakke, *Athanasius and Asceticism* (London: The John Hopkins University Press, 1998), p. 129.

at Tyre and again at Sardica, were trumped up.[48] According to Hilary of Poitiers, Athanasius distanced himself from Marcellus about this time.[49] To add to his sense of encouragement, a major programme of a church building was undertaken in Alexandria, at Athanasius's instigation.

However, in early 350 the Western emperor Constans was slain in a palace revolt and Constantius felt able to turn against Athanasius. Magnentius became emperor of the West, and Constantius, who was still preoccupied with the Persians, was forced to assure Athanasius that he would be the bishop 'in your own place for all time.'[50] But Athanasius was more loyal to the emperor than the emperor was to him. Sometime in 350, a legation from Magnentius may have made overtures to the Alexandrian patriarch but Athanasius refused to be swayed.[51] Athanasius acknowledged that he had met Constans—albeit not by himself[52]—but went on to claim that he had never met Magnentius, whom he called a tyrant and a traitor.[53] Magnentius was one who consulted the soothsayers, so it was unlikely that Athanasius would ever support him.

It was at this time that Athanasius was yet again tested. On 28 September 351, Constantius defeated Magnentius at Mursa, and the defeated general took his own life. Ursacius and Valens, whom Hanson calls 'two expert students of the imperial wind',[54] then renounced their recantations and turned against Athanasius.[55] In Athanasius's view, their first recantations in Rome were voluntary, whereas their repudiation of these recantations was

---

48.   Athanasius, *Defence Against the Arians* 58; Athanasius, *History of the Arians* 26.

49.   Joseph T. Lienhard, 'Marcellus of Ancyra in Modern Research,' *Theological Studies* 43, no. 3 (1982): p. 491.

50.   Barnes, *Athanasius and Constantius*, p. 104.

51.   Riall, 'Athanasius Bishop of Alexandria,' pp. 171–172.

52.   Athanasius, *Defence Before Constantius* 3, 6.

53.   Ibid., 6.

54.   Hanson, *Search for the Christian Doctrine of God*, p. 313.

55.   Athanasius, *History of the Arians* 29.

coerced.[56] Constantius also adopted a policy of trying to wean the Ethiopian Church away from its allegiance to Alexandria.

The decade of the creeds had begun, as the church wrestled for a Christological formula that most could accept. Over the next decade, Constantius convened at least nine church councils. In 351, the Council of Sirmium—an important city where, in fact, Constantius was born in 317—reaffirmed the decisions of the Eastern faction at Sardica, denounced the term *homoousios*, and condemned Athanasius, also charging him with treason. It passed 27 anathemas in all. In addition, it exiled Julius of Rome, Ossius of Cordova, and Hilary of Poitiers. In his *Defense of the Nicene Council*, written about 352–353, Athanasius vigorously defends the use of *homoousios*.

A council of bishops in Antioch in 352 may have been responsible for electing George of Cappadocia as bishop of Alexandria, whom Gibbon considers possibly to have become transformed into the St George legend![57] It would be difficult to find a candidate less auspicious and more inappropriate to become the patron saint of chivalry. Councils followed at Arles (late 353) and Milan (355), which came to similar conclusions in condemning Athanasius. Indeed, at Arles, Paulinus of Trier was exiled for supporting Athanasius. There were also Councils at Béziers (353), Sirmium (357, 358, 359), Constantinople (360), as well as the joint Council of Ariminum-Seleucia (359). This was indeed the age of church councils, so much so that the last great ancient Roman historian, Ammianus Marcellinus, who was a pagan, grumbled with respect to Constantius: 'Public transport hurried throngs of bishops hither and thither to attend what they call synods, and by his attempts to impose conformity Constantius only succeeded in hamstringing the post service.'[58] Apparently, traffic congestion and mail delays are not problems confined to the modern era!

56.   Ibid., 29.

57.   Gibbon, *History of the Decline and Fall*, 1:903.

58.   Ammianus Marcellinus, *The Later Roman Empire* (a.d.354–378), trans. by Walter Hamilton (London: Penguin, 2004), 21.16 (p. 232).

The Sirmium Council of 357 has come under scholarly scrut-iny and it has been suggested that Socrates's record is historically inaccurate. However, the confessions of the time all pointed in the same general direction, and that was along the lines that Socrates reported. Neither Arius nor Marcellus was condemned, but there was a strong emphasis on the inferiority of the Son.[59] Hilary famously called it the 'blasphemy of Sirmium'.[60] The term *homoiousios* was used, leading Edward Gibbon to mock 'the furious contests which difference of a single diphthong excited between the Homoousians and Homoiousians'.[61] Actually, it was an iota rather than a diphthong that constituted one of the differences, and the result was ambiguity in that 'of the same substance' can have the same meaning as 'of like substance'. In any case, as Hanson comments: 'Gibbon could never resist sacrificing history to epigram.'[62] After the joint council in 359 and the small Council of Constantinople, Jerome commented from Bethlehem: 'Down with the faith of Nicaea was the cry. The whole world groaned and was astonished to find itself Arian.'[63] Leo Davis states: 'The creed of Nicaea seemed to have gone down to defeat.'[64] Perhaps it might be fairer to say that the church councils were trying to avoid the extremes of Arius and of Marcellus and so managed to say nothing very definite.

The see of Antioch symbolized these divisions over the person of Christ. The Arians were led by Euzoïus, the Homoiousians (often called Homoeousians), who held that the Son was *homoiousios* with the Father (i.e. like the Father), by Melitius (supported by Basil of Caesarea), and the Nicenes by Paulinus (consecrated by Lucifer of Cagliari and later supported

59. Socrates, *Church History* 2.30.

60. Hilary of Poitiers, *On the Councils* 10.

61. Gibbon, *History of the Decline and Fall*, 1:787.

62. Hanson, *Search for the Christian Doctrine*, p. 347.

63. Jerome, *Against the Luciferians* 19.

64. Leo Donald Davis, *The First Seven Ecumenical Councils* (325-787): *Their History and Theology* (1983 ed.; repr. Collegeville, MN: Michael Glazier, 1990), p. 100.

by Athanasius and the bishops of Rome). The complication in an already highly complex situation was the group, which held that the Son was *homoiousios* with the Father (like the Father). In the case of the Cappadocian Fathers, these held to Nicene theology without using, initially at least, Nicene terms. By 360, Basil of Caesarea was writing:

> The phrase 'like in essence', if it be read with the addition, 'without any difference', I accept as conveying the same sense as the homoousion, in accordance with the sound meaning of the homoousion ... I am myself for the homoousion, as being less open to improper interpretation.[65]

The broad Eusebian cause was unravelling, and there was a growing consensus regarding the worth of Nicene terminology to be used to affirm the full deity of Christ.

On the political front, Athanasius was forced to defend himself in an apologia to Constantius. He denied the four charges of trying to set Constans and Constantius against one another, colluding with Magnentius, celebrating Easter in an unfinished and unconsecrated church, and ignoring the imperial summons.[66] It is significant that in replying to the charge that he celebrated Easter in an unconsecrated church, Athanasius's defense was that the crowd was too great and the practice had biblical precedent (Ezra 3:6; Nehemiah 8).[67] Constantius has been characterized by Richard Rubenstein as 'a relatively easygoing ruler',[68] while Lewis Ayres, and Timothy Barnes maintain that 'within the fourth-century context Constantius was a fairly mild ruler'.[69] R. P. C. Hanson's conclusion is similar in that he regards Constantius as 'by the standard of the late

---

65.   Basil of Caesarea, *Letter* 9

66.   See Athanasius, *Defence Before Constantius*.

67.   Ibid., 14–18.

68.   Rubenstein, *When Jesus Became God*, p. 182.

69.   Ayres, *Nicaea and its Legacy*, p. 133.

Roman Emperors, tolerant and even at times merciful'.[70] For all his feted mildness, Constantius accused Athanasius of being 'a man who had come forth from the lowest dens of infamy', 'a pestilent fellow' who was convicted of 'the basest crimes', and one who deserved killing ten times over.[71]

Ammianus aimed to treat Constantius impartially, but portrayed him as one who became cruel and merciless if he thought his authority was being challenged: 'He was adept at making a mountain of mischief out of a molehill of evidence.'[72] Athanasius flattered Constantius as one who was gracious and religious,[73] but soon contended that he had no mind of his own and was regulated by the suggestions of others, and so was worse than Saul, Ahab, Pilate, and the Jews, and was the precursor of Antichrist.[74] The same pattern of praise to Constantius, then terrible disappointment concerning him, can be found in the writings of Hilary of Poitiers. Athanasius eventually saw something of Constantius in Daniel's vision of the one who would speak words against the Most High, and persecute the saints for a time (Dan. 7:25).[75]

Clergy loyal to Athanasius were liable to be exiled, and civil servants who failed to coerce bishops into compliance were threatened with fines. Julius's successor at Rome, Liberius (bishop from 352–366), continued to support the besieged patriarch, even in 355 when Constantius coerced the 300-strong council at Milan to condemn Athanasius. The few who supported Athanasius were exiled, including Liberius. However, Liberius then capitulated, subscribed the Sirmian decisions, and in 357 was allowed to return to Rome. This council at Sirmium outlawed the use of *homoousios* and *homoiousios*, hence the hostility exhibited to this council by

70. Hanson, *Search for the Christian Doctrine*, p. 321.

71. Athanasius, *Defence Before Constantius* 30.

72. Ammianus Marcellinus, *The Later Roman Empire* 21.16.

73. Athanasius, *To the Bishops of Egypt* 5.

74. Athanasius, *History of the Arians* 45, 68–70.

75. Ibid., 74.

the Nicene party. Aged almost a hundred, the venerable Ossius of Cordova signed under coercion. By this time, Ossius was 'in love with the tomb' in Hilary's view, or 'senile' in Hanson's view.[76]

Diogenes, a notarius, was sent to Alexandria by Constantius in order to remove Athanasius, with the help of Syrianus, the Roman commander of Alexandria. However, the plebs, the free land-owning citizens, in Alexandria rallied to Athanasius's cause. Diogenes spent about five frustrating months in the city before he withdrew on 23 December 355. About six weeks later, on 8 February 356, five thousand troops broke up Athanasius's vigil service. According to Athanasius, people were attacked while they were praying, virgins were stripped naked, and even the dead were mistreated and left to the dogs.[77] Athanasius had his deacon read a Psalm, presumably Psalm 136, and the people answered: 'For his steadfast love endures forever'. Then Athanasius made his escape, without leaving a forwarding address.[78]

In the midst of all these troubles, Athanasius had spent his time writing On the Nicene Definition of Faith and his Apology Against the Arians. According to Athanasius, the persecution unleashed by Constantius was more severe than that of Maximian. The agèd Ossius, whom Athanasius generously called 'that great old man' who is 'Abraham-like',[79] was forced to sign an ambiguous creed. Ossius's opinion, as relayed to the emperor Constantius, was that, 'For whatever they assert, it is not on account of Athanasius, but for the sake of their own heresy.'[80] In Athanasius's view, 'they who favour the Arian doctrines indeed have no king but Caesar'.[81] He mocked them for their obsequious attitude to Constantius: 'they who deny

---

76. Hanson, Search for the Christian Doctrine, p. 337.

77. Athanasius, Defence Before Constantius 27.

78. Athanasius, Defence of His Flight 24.

79. Athanasius, History of the Arians 42, 45.

80. Ibid., 44.

81. Ibid., 3.

that the Son is everlasting, have called him Eternal Emperor'.[82] Apparently, the irony escaped them.

Arianism—or what might be called such—was starting to fracture about this time. Aëtius of Antioch, Eunomius from Cappadocia (who became bishop of Cyzicus in 360), and the radical neo-Arians were saying that Christ was dissimilar to God. As a consequence, they became known as Anomoeans or Anomoians ('unlikes').[83] Hanson calls them neo-Arians,[84] while Ayres refers to them as Heterousians.[85] They considered that the Son was not exactly like the Father. The Father is ingenerate and complete without the Son. The Son was like the Father in will, but not in His being. Aëtius's disciple and Eunomius's friend, Eudoxius (bishop of Germanicia in Syria, then Antioch, then Constantinople) emphasized that the Father was inherently unknown. He portrayed the Father as totally self-existent and complete without the Son. More moderate Arians were offended at this and some who had supported *homoiousios* were starting to see that they had common ground with those who upheld the *homoousios* of Nicaea. In his *Defence of the Nicene Definition*, Athanasius showed both his flexibility and his growing conviction that Nicene terminology was less ambiguous than any other. He challenged the Eusebians: 'if they hold the sense of the Council they will fully accept the terms in which it is conveyed'.[86]

Meanwhile, in the late 350s, Constantius exiled Aëtius, Eunomius and Eudoxius for saying that Christ is unlike God, and Basil of Ancyra and his followers for saying that Christ is like him.[87] Ayres does not consider this a volte-face on Constantius's

82. Athanasius, *Councils of Ariminum and Seleucia* 3.

83. Cf. Epiphanius, *Panarion* 76.

84. Hanson, *Search for the Christian Doctrine*, p. 598.

85. Ayres, *Nicaea and its Legacy*, p. 145.

86. Athanasius, *Defence of the Nicene Definition* 21.

87. Sozomen, *Church History* 4.14; Hanson, *Search for the Christian Doctrine*, p. 357.

part,[88] and indeed it may indicate a political ruler's desire for theological peace as much as anything. For all that, the Arian-leaning clergy had taken charge of many churches, while those in communion with Athanasius were banished to the desert.[89]

The 'Invisible Patriarch' in the Desert: The Third Exile (356–362)

This third exile suffered by Athanasius did not lead to his seeing the world, as did the first two exiles. He remained relatively nearby and used his time to produce his most extensive literary output. Down through the ages, deserts, like prisons, have proved to be productive sites for Christian writing. The cisterns of Alexandria were used as air-raid shelters in World War II, and it is possible that Athanasius spent some time at least hiding amongst them.

George the Cappadocian was appointed to succeed Athanasius. He had apparently amassed a fortune as a military contractor, and possessed a fine private library, although the orthodox regarded him as ignorant. Edward Gibbon viewed him as one who 'raised himself by the talents of a parasite' by flattering compliant patrons.[90] The pagan historian, Ammianus Marcellinus, described him as 'a human snake, who had often made them [i.e. the people of Alexandria] suffer from his poisonous fangs'.[91] Athanasius portrays him as one who worshiped idols and who possessed the temper of a hangman.[92] Whatever the case, George could not speak Coptic and seemed to be a committed Arian. Ammianus does not portray him as committed to anything and adds that, in informing on his fellow Alexandrians to the emperor Constantius, 'he forgot the faith he professed, which preaches only justice and mercy'.[93]

---

88.   Ayres, *Nicaea and its Legacy*, p. 153.

89.   Athanasius, *History of the Arians* 71–72.

90.   Gibbon, *History of the Decline and Fall*, 1:901.

91.   Ammianus Marcellinus, *The Later Roman Empire* 22.11.

92.   Athanasius, *To the Bishops of Egypt* 7.

93.   Ammianus Marcellinus, *The Later Roman Empire* 22.11.

Predictably, there were riots and an occupation of churches on 12-14 June 356, including the newly-renovated Great Church in the Caesarion, which had once proclaimed the deity of the dying emperors. Virgins had their heads exposed and were assailed with foul language and obscenities. Church furniture was set alight and there was much pillaging and looting.[94] The Arians encouraged the pagans and were worse than the pagans had been during the Great Persecution.[95] Only on 24 February 357 was George able to enter Alexandria, a move which provoked further riots. George had clergy and virgins arrested, and on 18 May 357, those loyal to Athanasius were attacked by soldiers in a cemetery. Athanasius deemed it prudent to retreat to Upper Egypt, where he may have spent much of his time in a dry cistern. A virgin of the church also seems to have protected him. Yet the violence continued intermittently, so much so that from October 358 to November 361 George himself remained outside Alexandria, attending church councils.

Himself under threat of capital punishment, Athanasius called on his bishops to remain firm. Athanasius was to spend six years in the desert, where he must have moved about constantly. Like Cyprian of Carthage during the Decian persecution of 249-250, Athanasius's flight attracted its critics and Athanasius felt obliged to defend his actions against charges of cowardice. Citing Jacob's flight from Esau, Moses's from Pharaoh, David's from Saul, and, more tenuously, Elijah's from Jezebel, he exercised his gift for sarcasm, suggesting of his critics: 'Perhaps they have not read these histories as being out of date.'[96] He piled up many more references—an indication, perhaps, that

---

94. Athanasius, *History of the Arians* 54-63.

95. Ibid., 55, 64. Christopher Haas points out that the pagans were a diverse group, and not monolithic; see his *Alexandria in Late Antiquity* (London: The John Hopkins University Press, 1997), pp. 131, 134. True enough, but Athanasius was speaking generally, not writing a sociological analysis for later historians.

96. Athanasius, *Defence of His Flight* 11.

he was feeling aggrieved by the criticisms. He pointed to
Matthew 10:23; 24:15-20; Ecclesiastes 7:17; Genesis 28:2;
Hebrews 11:37-38; 1 Samuel 26:10-11, and to Christ's own
flights in Matthew 2:13 and 12:15; also John 8:58-59 and
11:53-54. In any case, he blamed George of Cappadocia for
the violence and declared that 'if it be a bad thing to flee, it
is much worse to persecute'.[97]

The bishop was also a pastor and he sought to encourage
his people and wrote regarding the Arians' possession of the
churches, which he calls 'the places':

> For they hold the places, but you the Apostolic Faith. They are,
> it is true, in the places, but outside of the true Faith; while you
> are outside the places indeed, but the Faith, within you. Let us
> consider what is the greater—the place or the Faith. Clearly the
> true Faith. Who then has lost more, or who possesses more? He
> who holds the place, or he who holds the Faith? Good indeed
> is the place, when the Apostolic Faith is preached there, holy
> is it if the Holy One dwells there. But you are blessed, who by
> faith are in the Church.

He added: 'For if ever God shall give back the churches (for we
think he will) yet without such restoration of the churches the
Faith is sufficient for us.'[98] He pointed out that the Babylonians
gained the temple in Jerusalem, but it did them no good.

During this time, Athanasius was the hermit and the
'invisible patriarch'. He seems to have paid furtive visits to
Alexandria to encourage his flock and some officials must have
given him support. The church in Egypt gave him outstanding
support. At least one virgin, Eudaemonis, was tortured for
information as to Athanasius's whereabouts. The monks too
offered significant support. In fact, when Antony died, he left
his well-worn sheepskin cloak to be returned to Athanasius.
As we have seen, Pachomius became a strong supporter of

---

97. Ibid., 8.

98. Athanasius, *Letter* 29, fragment (slightly altered).

Athanasius, so Athanasius was upheld by the respective leaders of both brands of monasticism—the hermit style of Antony and the communal style of Pachomius. This was quite an achievement in an age where monastic suspicion of ordained clerics could be quite intense.

Athanasius probably wrote his popular *Life of Antony* about this time, a work that Derwas Chitty calls 'the first great manifesto of the monastic ideal'.[99] He also continued to write against the Arians, and considered those who called them Christians to be in great and grievous error; Arians were not to be called Christians but heretics who assault Christ.[100] However, he also continued to urge what he always had, that 'it beseems us to pray for all those that are in error'.[101] 'Right indeed is it to pity their dupes; well is it to weep over them.'[102] For all his involvement in conflict, Athanasius hardly speaks as one who was a bully and a gangster.

The Homoian bishops like Acacius (or Akakius) of Caesarea and Eudoxius of Antioch (originally of Germanica in Armenia, then of Antioch in 357-360, then Constantinople from 360 to 370) were starting to trigger off a reaction against themselves. They used *like* without further qualification and rejected any language of 'essence' (*ousia*), and so lacked theological precision. They reached the high point of their influence with the Niké/Constantinople Creed of 360: 'We declare that the Son is like the Father as the divine scriptures declare and teach.' This was designed to replace all previous creeds, including that of Nicaea, but such brevity tended to undermine their credibility. Many of the Homoians did not regard themselves as Arians, but they had become more hostile to Nicaea and this tended to make Nicaea more significant in responding to attacks on it. Accordingly, Athanasius began to make the Nicene terminology more central

99.   Derwas J. Chitty, *The Desert a City* (1966 ed.; repr. Oxford: Mowbrays, 1977), p. 2.

100. Athanasius, *Four Discourses Against the Arians* I.7.

101. Athanasius, *On the Opinion of Dionysius* 27.

102. Athanasius, *Four Discourses Against the Arians* 2.43.

to his understanding, albeit without losing sight of those who agreed with him in fundamentals but not in terminology.

Athanasius also warned against the Sabellians and those who saw the Spirit as a creature. He had not dealt with the person of the Spirit in his earlier works, but increasingly he came to argue that the Spirit is divine because only a divine person can sanctify. The last decade or so of Athanasius's life saw a controversy with those variously called Macedonians or *Pneumatomachi* ('Spirit fighters') or *Tropici* ('Trope mongers') who rejected the Godhead of the Holy Spirit.[103] The Macedonians took their name, probably unfairly in the view of R. P. C. Hanson,[104] from Macedonius, the bishop of Constantinople from 342 to about 360 when he was deposed, albeit not for heresy. As C. R. B. Shapland puts it: 'The question of the Spirit arose out of the question of the Son. It was a crisis within a crisis.'[105] Yet, as Kevin Hill shows, Athanasius possessed an understanding of the Holy Spirit from the beginning of his clerical life and well before the controversy broke out.[106] In Athanasius's view, the Arians and the Tropici were similar in that they 'maintain the same blasphemy against the holy Triad'.[107]

Sometime between 358 and 360, Athanasius became more involved in the controversy over the deity of the Spirit.[108] From

---

103. See the following for more on the Pneumatomachians. Michael A. G. Haykin, The Spirit of God: *The Exegesis of 1 and 2 Corinthians in the Pneumatomachian Controversy of the Fourth Century, Supplements to Vigiliae Christianae* 27 (Leiden: Brill, 1994); Athanasius the Great and Didymus the Blind, *Works on the Spirit*, trans. Mark DelCogliano, Andrew Radde-Gallwitz, and Lewis Ayres, Popular Patristics Series 43 (Yonkers, NY: St. Vladimir's Seminary Press, 2011).

104. Hanson, *Search for the Christian Doctrine*, p. 762.

105. Athanasius, *The Letters of Saint Athanasius Concerning the Holy Spirit* (trans. by C. R. B. Shapland [London: Epworth Press, 1951]), pp. 34-35.

106. Kevin Douglas Hill, *Athanasius and the Holy Spirit* (Minneapolis, MN: Fortress Press, 2016), p. xiv. Naturally, his doctrine of the Spirit developed (see pp. 64-65, 98-99).

107. Athanasius, *Concerning the Holy Spirit*, Letter 1.1.

108. For the dating, see Athanasius, *Concerning the Holy Spirit*, 16-18.

the desert,[109] presumably Nitria or further south to the lower Thebaid, Athanasius argued, 'If he makes men divine, it is not to be doubted that his nature is of God.'[110] A creature cannot save another creature, so in order to deify sinners, both the Son and the Spirit must be divine. If the Arians made Christ a created son, the Tropici rendered the Spirit a grandson![111]

Constantius was keen that a general council solve the impasse. After an earthquake in Nicomedia killed its bishop, Cecropios, Constantius called for a Western synod in Ariminum (Rimini) in Italy and moved the proposed Eastern synod from Nicomedia to Seleucia in Isauria. Ultimately, a Western council of about four hundred met at Ariminum in Italy in July 359 and an Eastern council of about one hundred and sixty met in Seleucia in September 359. This was a repeat of the joint Council of Serdica about sixteen years before this and almost as farcical. The majority of the Western council opposed any tampering with the Nicene Creed,[112] but Constantius welcomed the delegates of the minority position. This repudiated *homoousios* and *homoiousios*, but also anathematized 'unlike'.[113] Under considerable imperial coercion, representatives of both councils subscribed the new imperial Homoian creed on 31 December 359 or early 360 at Constantinople.

The Ariminum/Seleucia creed confessed the Son of God as the one who 'before all ages, and before all origin, and before all conceivable time, and before all comprehensible essence, was begotten impassibly from God ... whose origin no one knows save the Father alone who begat him'. It concluded by saying that the term 'essence' (*ousia*) had given offence as being misconceived by the people and as not a biblical word. It was not to be used of God again, because

109. Ibid., Letter 1.1, 1.33.

110. Ibid., Letter 1.24.

111. Athanasius, *Concerning the Holy Spirit*, Letter 4.4.

112. Athanasius, *Councils of Ariminum and Seleucia* 10.

113. Ibid., 29.

the divine Scriptures nowhere use it of Father and Son. 'But we say that the Son is like the Father in all things, as also the Scriptures say and teach.'[114] To Athanasius, this was, from one angle, not far from the kingdom of God, for 'the Image of the unalterable God must be unchangeable'.[115] However, he also saw dishonesty at work,[116] and charged that 'the aim of the present Councils was not truth, but the annulling of the acts of Nicaea'.[117]

> So the Godhead of the Son is the Father's; whence also it is indivisible, and; thus there is one God and none other but he. And so, since they are one, and the Godhead itself one, the same things are said of the Son, which are said of the Father, except his being said to be Father.[118]

In Athanasius's view, the language of likeness was not discarded, for 'the likeness of the Emperor in the image is exact, so that a person who looks at the image, sees in it the Emperor'.[119]

Although Athanasius was surviving in the Egyptian desert, he was not cut off from the outside world. He learned of the capitulation of Ossius of Cordova at the Council of Sirmium (in the modern Balkans) in October 357, where he (Ossius) held communion with Valens, Ursacius, and their ilk.[120] He also learned of the Councils of Ancyra in 358, Sirmium in 359, and Ariminum/Seleucia in 359. Athanasius saw the persecution in apocalyptic terms: 'It was an insurrection of impiety against godliness; it was zeal for the Arian heresy, and a prelude to the coming of Antichrist, for whom Constantius is thus preparing the way.'[121] To Athanasius,

---

114. Ibid., 8; Socrates, *Church History* 2.37.

115. Athanasius, *Four Discourses Against the Arians* 1.36.

116. Athanasius, *Councils of Ariminum and Seleucia* 9.

117. Ibid., 7.

118. Athanasius, *Four Discourses Against the Arians* 3.4.

119. Ibid., 3.5.

120. Athanasius, *History of the Arians* 45.

121. Ibid., 46.

the emperor had no warrant to rule the church.[122] The situation was threatening: 'Where is there a Church which now enjoys the privilege of worshipping Christ freely?'[123]

Then news reached Alexandria on 30 November 361 of the death of Constantius—he had died of fever, having been baptized by Euzoïus, and leaving no children, although his pregnant wife was to give birth to a daughter, who grew up to marry the emperor Gratian. Alexandria became restive again. George and two of his associates were arrested, and then they were lynched by the plebs on 24 December 361. George may have been beaten to death. His body was placed on a camel for a parade and then burned—cremation being the final indignity.[124] In his place, the Arians consecrated Lucius as bishop of Alexandria. Philostorgius claims that Athanasius orchestrated all the violence against George, and Timothy Barnes typically writes that it is highly unlikely that Athanasius's supporters were mere spectators.[125] Rubenstein too imagines Athanasius concluding that 'distasteful as popular violence may be, the Alexandrian crowd on that occasion had done the Lord's work'.[126] However, imagining history is not the same as recording history. Even the new emperor, Julian, an avowed enemy of the Christian faith, saw the riot as a pagan response to Christian attacks on the Mithraeum in Alexandria.[127]

'A Small Cloud': The Fourth Exile by the Banks of the Nile (362–364)

With the accession of Constantius's cousin, Julian (known to history as Julian the Apostate), in 361, Athanasius was able to return to Alexandria in 362, after an absence of nearly seven

---

122. Ibid., 52.

123. Ibid., 53.

124. For example, Epiphanius, *Panarion* 76.1.1-4.

125. Barnes, *Athanasius and Constantius*, p. 155.

126. Rubenstein, *When Jesus Became God*, p. 14.

127. See Ammianus, *The Later Roman Empire* 22.11 (pp.246-47); Julian, *Letter* 21; Gregory of Nazianzus, *Oration 21, On the Great Athanasius* 26.

years. He received a jubilant welcome and Gregory of Nazianzus rather inappropriately compared his entry to that of Jesus entering Jerusalem on a colt.[128] He was 'both peaceable and a peacemaker'[129] and treated those who injured him 'mildly and gently'.[130]

Raised a Christian, Julian had turned on the faith and decided that sunlight brought his mind into a state of ecstasy, that human beings need to recognise their divinity and that a true philosopher showed no interest in food, wine, or sex.[131] Julian wrote *Against the Galileans* in three books, which have only partially survived, where he objected to what he saw as the 'deification' of Jesus. However, he apparently had no objections to his own deification and in his own lifetime altars were set up in his honor.[132] Indeed, the ancient sacrifices were resumed with much vigor—or indulgence—and Christian teachers were debarred from the schools. Until an earthquake put an end to his plans, Julian wanted to rebuild the temple in Jerusalem, thinking that this would cause the Christians some consternation. With regard to Athanasius, he hoped that the return of the patriarch would be a disruptive influence on the church at Alexandria and that it would self-destruct. From about this time, or perhaps even 359, Athanasius sought to reconcile the *homoiousians* of Asia Minor, hitherto seen as a semi-Arian party, to the Nicene term *homoousios*.

In the second century, Irenaeus of Lyons had said that God has two hands—the Son and the Spirit.[133] Given this triadic vision of God even in the Old Testament (e.g. Isa. 48:16; Hag. 2:4-5), Athanasius argued, 'When the Spirit was with the people, God,

128. Gregory of Nazianzus, *Oration 21, On the Great Athanasius* 27-29.

129. Ibid., 36.

130. Ibid., 30.

131. Chadwick, *The Church in Ancient Society*, 298.

132. Ibid., pp. 306-307.

133. Irenaeus, *Against Heresies*, 4. Pref. 4.

through the Son in the Spirit, was with them'.[134] And 'when we partake of the Spirit we have the Son; and when we have the Son, we have the Spirit'.[135]

The Council of Alexandria met in 362—the month is unknown—and despite its relatively small size, achieved much. Among its members were Asterius of Petra, Eusebius of Vercelli, legates from Lucifer of Cagliari, Apollinaris of Laodicaea, and Paulinus who led the Eustathian community at Antioch. Flexibility in expression went hand-in-hand with precision in substance—and this reflected Athanasius's mindset. The council was conciliatory in seeking to clear up misunderstandings of 'person' (*hypostasis*) and 'substance' or 'essence' (*ousia*). The Homoiousians spoke of three hypostases, while the Nicenes of only one hypostasis. The Council at Alexandria agreed with both parties. Furthermore, the West used *hypostasis* to mean *ousia* but the East began to use it to mean 'person' (*prosōpon*). So, for example, Basil of Caesarea would speak of three *hypostases*. Gregory of Nazianzus came to consider that this was a result of the Latin language. He writes of the Westerners who could not distinguish between essence and *hypostasis* 'owing to the scantiness of their vocabulary, and its poverty of terms'. Hence, said Gregory, the Christian world could have been torn asunder in 'the strife about syllables'.[136]

In the third century, Dionysius of Alexandria had spoken of three *hypostases*, but his namesake at Rome considered that this was the equivalent of speaking of three gods. Hence, speaking in general terms, the East accused the West of Sabellianism, while the West was fearful that the East had embraced tritheism. Athanasius, as an Easterner, believed that those who held to three *hypostases* were Trinitarian.[137] He considered that the question of one *hypostasis* or three *hypostases* ought not to be

134. Athanasius, *Concerning the Holy Spirit*, Letter 1.12.

135. Ibid., Letter 4.4.

136. Gregory of Nazianzus, *Oration 21, On the Great Athanasius* 35.

137. Athanasius, *Tome or Synodal Letter to the People of Antioch* 5.

pressed too far.[138] Those, who had some qualms about the use of *homoousios*, still ought, in Athanasius's view, to accept the Nicene anathemas of Arianism.[139] With the squabbling Arians in mind, he lamented that some men have no motive except contentiousness,[140] and probably with Apollinaris of Laodicea in mind (in northern Syria, not in Asia Minor), he pointed out that Christ became true man, not just a body.[141] In theology, one's friends and pupils—notably, Apollinaris and Marcellus—can make life almost as difficult as can one's opponents. Most movingly, Athanasius wrote, or prayed: 'Perhaps God will have pity on us, and unite what is divided, and, there being once more one flock, we shall all have one leader, even our Lord Jesus Christ.'[142] The Council at Alexandria made four demands: that Arianism be condemned; Nicaea be accepted; those who say the Spirit is a creature be condemned; and that the heresies of Sabellius, Paul of Samosata, Valentinus, Basilides, and the Manichaeans be repudiated.

Not long before the Council of Alexandria in 362, Hilary of Poitiers had defended the Nicene Creed that Father, Son, and Holy Spirit were one in substance (*homoousios*), but he acknowledged, 'The expression contains both a conscientious conviction and the opportunity for delusion.'[143] Indeed, he asked: 'Some misunderstand *homoousios*; does that prevent me from understanding it?'[144] Athanasius too was convinced that Nicene terminology was biblically defensible and accurate: 'neither are the terms of the Fathers faulty, but profitable to those who

---

138. Ibid., 6.

139. Athanasius, *To the Bishops of Africa* 9.

140. Athanasius, *Tome or Synodal Letter to the People of Antioch* 5.

141. Athanasius, *Tome or Synodal Letter to the People of Antioch* 7. R. P. C. Hanson thinks that Athanasius had Arianism in mind here, not Apollinarianism, but that is unlikely (Hanson, *Search for the Christian Doctrine*, p. 647).

142. Athanasius, *Tome or Synodal Letter to the People of Antioch* 8.

143. Hilary of Poitiers, *On the Councils* 67.

144. Ibid., 86, altered.

honestly read and subversive of all irreligion, though the Arians so often burst with rage at being condemned by them'.[145]

Athanasius's tone could be very firm, but also measured and humble. He could also explode at what he called 'the vomit of the heretics'.[146] Yet in dealing with Acts 2:36, which says that God *made* Jesus Lord and Christ, Athanasius wrote that 'he made' means 'he manifested'. Then he added rather mildly: 'This, at least according to my nothingness, is the meaning of this passage.'[147] He was not one to contend for terminology if the meaning were preserved. He was no blinkered fanatic and wrote with understanding and magnanimity: 'Nor do we here attack them as Ariomaniacs, nor as opponents of the Fathers, but we discuss the matter with them as brothers with brothers, who mean what we mean, and dispute only about the word.'[148] He urged: 'Let us not fight with shadows'.[149] Showing the same spirit of flexibility, he cited Paul on not contending about words (2 Tim. 2:14) and about being all things to all men (1 Cor. 9:22).[150] Later, Augustine of Hippo could write in this same spirit when he discussed the word 'person' (*prosōpon*). Augustine stated that 'when the question is asked, What three?, human language labours altogether under great poverty of speech. The answer, however, is given three "persons", not that it might be (completely) spoken, but that it might not be left (wholly) unspoken.'[151]

Athanasius was not one who delighted in being controversial for its own sake,[152] and so he could write to Diodorus of Tyre to 'enter upon no controversy with the heretics, but overcome their

145. Athanasius, *Councils of Ariminum and Seleucia* 34.

146. Athanasius, *Four Discourses Against the Arians* 2.30.

147. Ibid., 2.15.

148. Athanasius, *Councils of Ariminum and Seleucia* 41.

149. Ibid., 54.

150. Athanasius, *Epistles* 62 and 63.

151. Augustine, *On the Holy Trinity* 5.9.

152. Athanasius, *Concerning the Holy Spirit*, Letter 1.1.

argumentativeness with silence, their ill-will with courtesy'.[153]
This counters Ammianus Marcellinus's record of the views of
Julian: 'Experience had taught him that no wild beasts are such
dangerous enemies to man as Christians are to one another.'[154]
Yet all was not peace and light. Marcellus supported the Synod
of Alexandria, but Basil of Caesarea was rather violent in his
opposition to Marcellus.[155] Henry Chadwick comments: 'It was
harder to reconcile rival bishops than rival creeds.'[156] This was
true enough at times, but it is not a fair assessment of Athanasius.
In any case, Basil was to warm to Athanasius whom he referred
to as 'the one consolation left to us in our troubles'.[157]

According to Robert Riall, the Egyptian bishops had split
down the middle, with about half being exiled and half cooperating with the civil authorities.[158] Again, Athanasius
showed his magnanimity, as he was not harsh on those who had
co-operated with his enemies. All they had to do was confess
the creedal formula of Nicaea. All through his life, Athanasius
set out no elaborate system of penance for those who turned
from alternative theologies to embrace that confessed at Nicaea.
Regarding the Tropici, for example, he wrote: 'Perhaps, even
by a late repentance, they may wash away from their souls the
perversity which formerly was in them.'[159]

Athanasius was also hoping that a conciliatory approach
might resolve the divisions in the church at Antioch where the
Arian bishop Euzoïus had confronted two rivals, Eustathius and
Meletius. Athanasius wrote to the people of Antioch, urging

153. Athanasius, *Epistle 64*.

154. Ammianus Marcellinus, *The Later Roman Empire* 22.5 (p.239).

155. Joseph T. Lienhard, 'Marcellus of Ancyra in Modern Research,' *Theological Studies* 43, no. 3 (1982): 500. See Basil's *Epistle 69* to Athanasius which Athanasius seems to have ignored

156. Chadwick, *The Church in Ancient Society*, p. 294.

157. Basil of Caesarea, *Letter 80*.

158. Riall, 'Athanasius Bishop of Alexandria,' 232n13.

159. Athanasius, *Concerning the Holy Spirit*, Letter 3.7.

the followers of Meletius (the Homoiousians) to unite with 'our beloved Paulinus',[160] a successor to Eustathius. Athanasius's history was against him, as he had favored Eustathius whereas Basil of Caesarea had favored Meletius. Whatever the case, the two sides missed the opportunity to unite.

The serious and philosopher-impersonating Julian, who grew a wispy beard and wore the long hair of a philosopher, did not take long to act. He cut taxes, attacked Christians, and looked back to the days of Alexander the Great as a golden era. Rather ingenuously, he explained that exiled bishops could return to their countries, not their sees. This interpretation was motivated by his fear that, if left unmolested, Athanasius would soon restore Nicene orthodoxy and a considerable measure of unity to the church in Egypt. Athanasius's supporters petitioned Julian, but Julian responded on 23 October 362 by exiling Athanasius from Egypt, not just Alexandria. In a wild letter to Ecdicius, the prefect of Egypt, Julian fumed:

> I swear by mighty Serapis that, if Athanasius the enemy of the gods does not depart from that city, or rather from all Egypt, before the December Kalends, I shall fine the cohort which you command a hundred pounds of gold … By all the gods there is nothing I should be so glad to see, or rather hear reported as achieved by you, as that Athanasius has been expelled beyond the frontiers of Egypt. Infamous man! He has had the audacity to baptise Greek women of rank during my reign! Let him be driven forth![161]

Death seemed as likely as exile to Athanasius at this time. Theodoret records a marvelous story that while Athanasius was fleeing down the Nile in a boat, his pursuers drew near to the boat and inquired: 'How far off is Athanasius?' Since he was not recognized, Athanasius replied: 'Not far.'[162] And so Athanasius was able to escape.

160. Athanasius, *Tome or Synodal Letter to the People of Antioch* 3.

161. Julian, *Letter* 46 .

162. Theodoret, *Church History* 3.5.

Athanasius does not seem to have been unduly worried by all this and referred to it as 'a small cloud which will soon pass'.[163] He proved to be prophetic, and, in fact, his fourth and fifth exiles were both relatively brief. Athanasius withdrew to Chereu, south of Alexandria, while two presbyters, Paulus and Astericius, were exiled to the Western Delta. In 363, Athanasius was forced further up the Nile.

Athanasius wrote his annual *Easter Letter* from Memphis in 363, then went on to the Thebaid and to Thebes. Julian, meanwhile, was speared in the liver in a war with the Persians and, according to Theodoret, died while crying out: 'You have conquered, O Galilean!'[164] Legend or not, there was truth in the cry. Julian's successor, Jovian, entreated Athanasius to return. Athanasius had in fact left Egypt for a time in order to meet Jovian in Syria. Experience had taught Athanasius to be careful to arm himself with written documents.[165]

Prospects seemed bright, but three days after Athanasius arrived back in Alexandria in February 364, Jovian accidentally died of asphyxiation and Valentinian I (364–375) assigned the East to his Arian brother Valens (364–378). Again, Athanasius was sentenced into exile, but the sentence could not immediately be carried out due to riots in Alexandria in favor of Athanasius.

Final Years: Fifth Exile to Death (365–373)

When a devastating tidal tsunami hit the city on 21 June 365, Athanasius was still there to be involved in relief work. Ships were hurled by the returning sea and landed on the roofs of great buildings. Ammianus Marcellinus described it in graphic terms: 'a frightful disaster, surpassing anything related either in legend or authentic history, overwhelmed the whole world'.[166]

---

163. Ibid., 3.5; Sozomen, *Church History* 5.15.

164. Theodoret, *Church History* 3.20.

165. Athanasius, *Epistle 56*.

166. Ammianus Marcellinus, *The Later Roman Empire* 26.10 (p. 333).

On 5 October of that same year, troops came to arrest Athanasius but he had been forewarned and had fled. However, Athanasius was not the only one with troubles, and faced by the threat of the usurper Procopius in Constantinople, which threw the East into a panic, Valens granted Athanasius the guarantee he desired on 1 February 366.

This exile probably only lasted for four or five months. By this time, many of the Western bishops had renounced the Ariminum Creed of 359 and adopted that of Nicaea. In 356 Athanasius was an isolated figure in the east, but by 362 he was an elder statesman.[167] There were setbacks, but Athanasius's position seemed to be strengthening. In Alexandria itself, he was behind the conversion of the temple of Bendis into a church building in September 369 and took over the complex of buildings known as the Caesarion, which had been taken from the pagans and given by Constantius to Gregory of Cappadocia, but which came to be used by the church faithful to Nicaea.[168]

With the empire under increasing pressure, Valens could not risk its chief granary and source of tax revenues to remain in unfriendly hands. This exile, by Valens, was brief and Athanasius concealed himself for four months in his father's tomb (October 365–February 366).[169] On his return, Athanasius toured Upper Egypt and attracted large demonstrations of support. Athanasius's Arian rival, Lucius, was increasingly frustrated and in need of imperial protection. Support for Arianism, however one defines it, was collapsing, but its demise was not quite at hand. After Athanasius's death, Valens continued to hound his successor, Peter, who fled to Rome until Valens's own death in 378.

During this time in the 360s, Athanasius was able to appoint bishops, many of whom were drawn from the monasteries.

167. Barnes, *Athanasius and Constantius*, p. 152.

168. See Haas, *Alexandria in Late Antiquity*, 210; Epiphanius, *Panarion* 69.2.3.

169. Socrates, *Church History* 4.13.

Basil of Caesarea had also been appointing pro-Nicene clergy throughout Asia Minor. In all his trials, Athanasius looked especially to the Psalms for comfort and wisdom. He saw in them history and prophecies but also 'the emotions of the soul'.[170] More than that, they were like a mirror to the person singing them, for 'the Book of Psalms possesses somehow the perfect image for the soul's course of life'.[171]

Athanasius may have taken up his pen against Apollinarianism, but not against Apollinaris, and he died convinced of his friend's orthodoxy.[172] For a man whose life had been, in Dean Milman's words, 'one unwearied and incessant strife',[173] Athanasius at least died in peace on 2-3 May 373. Five days before his death, he had chosen Peter as his successor and he was consecrated. Peter was soon forced to flee to Rome, for the battle for Nicaea was not yet won. C. Wilfred Griggs notes: 'The Arian takeover after Athanasius's death signifies that the success of his consolidation efforts was due more to the strength of his position and personality than to his achieving doctrinal or ecclesiastical unity among the Christians.'[174] Actually, it signifies no more than that the emperor Valens was Arian-leaning.

In 378, Valens perished in a massacre of the Roman legions of the eastern empire by the Huns and Goths at the Battle of Hadrianopolis. Valens's body was never found. Gratian appointed Theodosius as emperor of the East. Theodosius had a policy of 'No heretics' and, at the Council of Constantinople

---

170. Athanasius, *Letter to Marcellinus* 10.

171. Ibid., 12, 14.

172. Epiphanius, Panarion 77.2.1-7; Athanasius, *Epistle 59*. George D. Dragas, *Saint Athanasius of Alexandria: Original Research and New Perspectives* (Rollinsford, NH: Orthodox Research Institute, 2005), p. 150. Dragas considers Athanasius's two treatises against Apollinaris to be authentic, but that is not universally accepted.

173. Cited in R. Wheeler Bush, *St Athanasius: His Life and Times* (London: SPCK, 1888), 219.

174. C. Wilfred Griggs, *Early Egyptian Christianity from its Origins to 451 C.E.* (Leiden: Brill, 1988), p. 182.

in 381, Nicene orthodoxy was reaffirmed. The first president of the Council was Meletius of Antioch but he died soon after his appointment and Gregory of Nazianzus was elected in his place. But he soon resigned, going into voluntary exile, to be replaced by Nectarius, an unbaptized layman who quickly became the bishop of Constantinople.

Gregory of Nazianzus is famous in some circles for his vehement dislike of the machinations of church councils. In 382, he wrote as one who was weary of church and imperial politics:

> For my part, if I am to write the truth, my inclination is to avoid all assemblies of bishops, because I have never seen any Council come to a good end, nor turn out to be a solution of evils. On the contrary, it usually increases them. You always find there love of contention and love of power (I hope you will not think me a bore, for writing like this), which beggar description; and, while sitting in judgment on others, a man might well be convicted of ill-doing himself long before he should put down the ill-doings of his opponents. So I retired into myself; and came to the conclusion that the only security for one's soul lies in keeping quiet. Now, moreover, this determination of mine is supported by ill-health; for I am always on the point of breathing my last, and am hardly able to employ myself to any effect. I trust, therefore, that, of your generosity, you will make allowances for me, and that you will be good enough to persuade our most religious Emperor also not to condemn me for taking things quietly, but to make allowances for my ill-health. He knows how it was on this very account that he consented to my retirement, when I petitioned for this in preference to any other mark of his favour.[175]

The Council of Constantinople in his view was 'a flock of jackdaws combining together',[176] which needed to go further in defining the deity of the Spirit.[177]

---

175. Gregory of Nazianzus, *Epistle 130*.

176. Hanson, *Search for the Christian Doctrine*, p. 809.

177. Ibid., p. 819.

Arianism in all its variant forms did not die out immediately, for various Germanic peoples like the Burgundians and the Visigoths were still Arian. In 418–419 and again in 427–428, for instance, Augustine was drawn into debates with opponents who were Arian, or Homoean, in their theology. Indeed, the heresy never quite died out. Later, it was to haunt John Milton and Isaac Watts, capture Isaac Newton, and decimate eighteenth century English Presbyterianism.

The liberal Protestant, Adolf von Harnack regarded the victory of the Nicene Creed as 'a victory of the priests over the faith of the Christian people'.[178] But Nicene orthodoxy reflects the biblical truth that in Christ all the fullness of the Godhead dwells bodily (Col. 2:9). By the end of the fourth century, it had become the official creed of the Roman Empire. As for Athanasius's body, it was transferred later to Constantinople, then in 1454 to Venice.

---

178. Adolf von Harnack, *History of Dogma*, trans. Neil Buchanan (New York: Dover Publications, 1961), 4: 106.

6

'FOR HE BECAME MAN ...'

A Summary of Athanasius's Theology and Introduction to On the Incarnation *and* Against the Gentiles

General overview of On the Incarnation of the Word

Athanasius is probably best known for his treatise *On the Incarnation of the Word of God.* Here, in his own repetitive and relatively unphilosophical way, Athanasius attempted to expound how the eternal Word of God assumed flesh in order that humanity might become incorruptible. Essential to Athanasius's thought is the premise that only God can redeem what He has created. Therefore, the Word must be truly God, for a creature cannot join other creatures to God.[1] The classic expression of Athanasius's theology is his well-known declaration regarding the Son of God: 'For he became man that we might become divine; and he revealed himself through a body that we might receive an idea of the invisible Father; and he endured insults from men that we might inherit incorruption.'[2] David Gwynn complains that there is an ontological polarization of God and creation in Athanasius's theology.[3] There is, but this only reflects the teaching, for example, of the apostle Paul in Romans 1:18-32.

1.   Athanasius, *Against the Arians* 69.

2.   Athanasius, *On the Incarnation* 54.

3.   David M. Gwynn, *The Eusebians: The Polemic of Athanasius of Alexandria and the Construction of the 'Arian Controversy,'* Oxford Theological Monographs (Oxford: Oxford University Press, 2007), p. 246.

Athanasius wrote of the Word of God: 'He took to himself a body, and that not foreign to our own'.[4] The incarnation was thus in Athanasius's view a genuine one, for 'he [the Word] did not wish simply to be in a body, nor did he wish merely to appear, for if he had wished only to appear he could have made his theophany through some better means'.[5] To be somewhat anachronistic, it can be said that Athanasius worked within the bounds of what later became Chalcedonian orthodoxy, with Christ defined as true God and true man.

Athanasius considered himself inadequate as a theological writer,[6] and unpracticed in speech.[7] He never entered the fray as a detached academic philosopher. He was first and foremost a Christian, and his declared aim was that a right understanding of theology might strengthen faith in Christ, that 'you may have ever greater and stronger piety towards him'.[8]

The Dating of *On the Incarnation*

From at least the time of Bernard de Montfaucon in 1698, it has been traditional to date *Against the Gentiles* and *On the Incarnation of the Word* as one treatise, written about the year 318, before the outbreak of the Arian crisis. Archibald Robertson, for example, as the translator of Athanasius's works in the Schaff series of Nicene and Post-Nicene Fathers, held to this date.[9] This is also the view of William Bright,[10] Johannes Quasten,[11] Thomas F. Torrance,[12]

---

4.   Athanasius, *On the Incarnation* 8.

5.   Athanasius, *On the Incarnation* 8.

6.   Athanasius, *Epistle* 52.1, 2.

7.   Ibid., 29.12.

8.   Athanasius, *On the Incarnation* 1.

9.   A. Robertson, 'Introduction to the Treatise *Contra Gentes*,' in *Athanasius: Select Works and Letters* (NPNF2 4:1), page 1.

10. William Bright, 'Athanasius' in *A Dictionary of Christian Biography*, eds. William Smith and Henry Wace (London: John Murray, 1877), p. 181.

11. Johannes Quasten, *Patrology* (Westminster, CA: Christian Classics, 1986), 3:25.

12. Thomas F. Torrance, *The Trinitarian Faith* (Edinburgh: T&T Clark, 1988), p. 148.

George Dragas,[13] F. F. Bruce,[14] and the earlier Timothy Barnes.[15] This was because neither of Athanasius's works refer explicitly to the Arian controversy. However, it would also mean that they were written by a man who may not have been twenty years of age, if 318 is correct. At the other extreme is the view of H. Nordberg that they date from the years 361–363, during the reign of Julian the Apostate.[16] Nordberg's view is eccentric; it would mean that Athanasius did not use the term 'essence' (*ousia*) precisely at the time when he was most pressed for its use.

Another possibility is that Athanasius wrote them on the way to Nicaea in 325, or perhaps a little later, as Carl Beckwith,[17] Khaled Anatolios,[18] David Gwynn,[19] Thomas Weinandy, and the later Timothy Barnes[20] and suggest.[21] James Ernest considers that what he detects as a triumphalist tone means that the works come after 328 but before the setback at the Synod of Tyre in 335.[22] On the other hand, Charles Kannengiesser,[23] Frances

---

13. George D. Dragas, *Saint Athanasius of Alexandria: Original Research and New Perspectives* (Rollinsford, NH: Orthodox Research Institute, 2005), p. 194.

14. F. F. Bruce, *The Spreading Flame* (1958 ed.; repr. Exeter: Paternoster, 1976), pp. 304–305.

15. Timothy Barnes, *Constantine and Eusebius* (Cambridge, MA: Harvard University Press, 1981), p. 206.

16. H. Nordberg, 'A Reconsideration of the Date of St Athanasius' *Contra Gentes and De Incarnatione*' Studia Patristica 3 (1961): pp. 264, 266.

17. See Carl Beckwith, 'Athanasius,' in *Shapers of Christian Orthodoxy*, ed. Bradley G. Green (Nottingham: Apollos, 2010), 167n39.

18. Khaled Anatolios, *Athanasius: The Coherence of his Thought* (London: Routledge, 1998), p. 29 (for a date between 328 and 335).

19. David Gwynn, *Athanasius of Alexandria: Bishop, Theologian, Ascetic, Father*, Christian Theology in Context (Oxford: Oxford University Press, 2012), pp. 55, 65-66.

20. Barnes, *Athanasius and Constantius*, p. 13.

21. Thomas G. Weinandy, *Athanasius: A Theological Evaluation* (Aldershot: Ashgate, 2007), p. 3.

22. James D. Ernest, *The Bible in Athanasius of Alexandria*, Bible in Ancient Christianity 2 (Leiden: Brill, 2004), p. 45.

23. Charles Kannengiesser, 'Athanasius of Alexandria and the Foundation of Traditional Christology,' *Theological Studies* 34 (1973): 107.

Young,[24] Henry Chadwick,[25] R. P. C. Hanson,[26] Robert Riall,[27] and R. W. Thomson[28] consider that a yet later date is much more likely, perhaps while Athanasius was in exile at Trier in 335–337. Probability favors this dating, although not necessarily for the reasons that some scholars give. Hanson, for example, cynically suggests that he wrote about this time before he came to use Arianism as a smokescreen for his own episcopal maladministration.

Other considerations are more convincing. They are mature works and Athanasius in exile had some incentive not to be too provocative. A head-on confrontation with the Arians might easily become a head-on confrontation with a hot-tempered emperor. Athanasius was not always appreciated for his diplomacy, but he had some talents along those lines. Furthermore, Athanasius says that when he wrote, his teachers were not available to him,[29] which presumably means he could not take his library with him into exile. Athanasius was in the habit of using writers,[30] a common practice in the ancient world, so he may have meant that he labored without an amanuensis.

The Creator re-creates

True to Scripture, Athanasius was convinced that only the creator can be the redeemer.[31] The creation cannot produce its own savior and redeemer. In the prayer of Augustine of Hippo: 'What else can save us but your hand, remaking what

24. Frances Young, *From Nicaea to Chalcedon* (London: SCM, 1983), p. 69.

25. Henry Chadwick, *The Church in Ancient Society* (Oxford: Oxford University Press, 2003), pp. 228–229.

26. R. P. C. Hanson, *The Search for the Christian Doctrine of God: The Arian Controversy 318–381* (Edinburgh: T&T Clark, 1988), p. 418.

27. Robert Archie Riall, 'Athanasius Bishop of Alexandria: The Politics of Spirituality (Egypt)' (PhD dissertation, University of Cincinnati, 1987), pp. 91–92.

28. R. W. Thomson in *Athanasius, De Incarnatione* (Oxford: Clarendon, 1971), p. xxiii.

29. Athanasius, *Against the Gentiles* 1.

30. Athanasius, *Defence Before Constantius* 11.

31. See, for instance, Isaiah 40–66, notably 45:18, 21–22; Colossians. 1:15–20.

you have made?"[32] To Athanasius, as to the Bible, the author of creation is also the author of re-creation. Even when some of his detailed exegesis seems less than convincing, this big picture—the metanarrative of creation, fall, and redemption—faithfully reproduces the message of the Bible.

The Word has to be divine because only the creator could recreate the creation, suffer for all, and represent all to the Father.[33] Parallel to this is the notion that 'creature does not worship creature'.[34] Near the end of his life, Athanasius summed up his thesis that 'a creature could never be saved by a creature, any more than the creatures were created by a creature if the Word was not creator'.[35]

Athanasius centers on the person of Christ in the context of redemption. He thus writes of Christ, as He pays the debt for sinners:

> Since the debt owed by all men had still to be paid, for all ... had to die, therefore after the proof of his divinity given by his works, he now on behalf of all men offered the sacrifice and surrendered his own temple to death on behalf of all, in order to make them all guiltless and free from the first transgression, and to reveal himself superior to death, showing his own incorruptible body as first-fruits of the universal resurrection.[36]

His soteriology was not simply centered on the incarnation, or even the incarnation and the resurrection, although J. N. D. Kelly rightly sees this as the dominant strain in his approach.[37] Indeed, Athanasius could interpret the cross almost in resurrection terms: 'The Cross has been not a disaster, but a

---

32. Augustine, *Confessions* 5.7.

33. Athanasius, *On the Incarnation* 7.

34. Athanasius, *Four Discourses Against the Arians* 2.23.

35. Athanasius, *Epistle* 60.8.

36. Athanasius, *On the Incarnation* 20. See also *On the Incarnation* 9.2; 20.2; 20.5; 25.2.

37. J. N. D. Kelly, *Early Christian Doctrines* (5th ed.; London: Adam and Charles Black, 1977), pp. 377-380.

healing of Creation'.[38] Furthermore, 'it was demonstrated to all that the body had not died through the weakness of the nature of the Word who dwelt in it, but in order that death might be destroyed in it through the power of the Saviour'.[39]

In Athanasius's view, the Son took 'a body pure and truly unalloyed by intercourse with men'[40]–hence the Virgin Birth was necessary. He went on: 'And thus taking a body like ours, since all were liable to the corruption of death, and surrendering it to death on behalf of all, he offered it to the Father.'[41] The cross soon gives way to the resurrection, as he suggests 'by the grace of the resurrection', and the Word rid men of death 'as straw is destroyed by fire'.[42] To Athanasius, 'man is by nature mortal in that he was created from nothing'.[43]

The nature of the atonement

Athanasius could at times sound quite Augustinian, or at least anti-Pelagian: 'It is indeed impossible to make an adequate return to God; still, it is a wicked thing for us who receive the gracious gift, not to acknowledge it.'[44] He went on to tell his flock in his *Easter Letter* for 333: 'Let us be sensible of the gift, though we are found insufficient to repay it'.[45] Because of our sin–'there is no one free from defilement, though his course may have been but one hour on the earth'[46]–our works can only be a response to God's grace. Hence, 'when we render a recompense to the Lord to the utmost of our power ... we give nothing of our own,

---

38. Athanasius, *Againt the Gentiles* 1. Note John 12:31 and Col. 2:15 for the cross as victory.

39. Athanasius, *On the Incarnation* 26.

40. Ibid., 8.

41. Ibid., 8.

42. Ibid., 8.

43. Ibid., 4.

44. Athanasius, *Easter Letter* 5.3.

45. Ibid., 5.3.

46. Ibid., 5.6.

but those things which we have before received from him, this being especially of his grace, that he should require, as from us, his own gifts'.[47]

For Athanasius, redemption meant incorruption, for the enemy was death as much as sin. Hence the focus was on the incarnation and the resurrection rather than the crucifixion and the atonement. In a certain sense, he viewed the incarnation as the redemption and Christ's person as His work. On occasions, Athanasius would write of substitutionary atonement, as when he stated that Christ had become a curse for us[48] and that He had taken upon Himself the judgment.[49] However, the general emphasis lies not on Christ's payment of our debt to God, but on the claim that 'the incorruptible Son of God was united to all men by his body similar to theirs'.[50] Although Athanasius never made it clear how it could be so, he believed that by assuming one body, the Word was present with all, and somehow humanity was swept up into the deity.

Corruption rather than guilt was the enemy: 'If there had been only a trespass, and not a consequent corruption, repentance would have been sufficient.'[51] Repentance is apparently enough to take away guilt, but more is needed to undo our corruption and mortality. It would be fair to say that Athanasius saw Christ more as an equivalent person rather than as one who paid an equivalent penalty.

In George Dragas's view, Athanasius implies that the debt that the Savior paid at Calvary was to the devil rather than to God, although he quickly qualifies this to say that both are true.[52] In some ways Anselm's *Why God Became Man* came over seven

---

47. Ibid., 5.4.

48. Athanasius, *Against the Arians* 3.33.

49. Ibid., 1.60.

50. Athanasius, *On the Incarnation* 9.

51. Ibid., 7.4.

52. G. D. Dragas, *Saint Athanasius of Alexandria: Original Research and New Perspectives* (Rollinsford, NH: Orthodox Research Institute, 2005), pp. 128-129.

hundred years too late for Athanasius, yet the Alexandrian bishop still spoke the language of substitution: 'For as by receiving our infirmities, he is said to be infirm himself, though not himself infirm, for he is the Power of God, and he became sin for us and a curse, though not having sinned himself, but because he himself bore our sins and our curse.'[53] Through the occasional Alexandrian haze, Athanasius perceived what the pagans did not, 'that the cross was not the ruin but the salvation of creation'.[54]

In Athanasius's theological scheme, the cross was portrayed more in terms of conflict rather than suffering. Christ's divinity is incommunicable but His perfect manhood is communicable. Just a few years before his death, Athanasius and his bishops wrote to the bishops of Africa: 'For we too, albeit we cannot become like God in essence, yet by progress in virtue imitate God, the Lord granting us this grace.'[55] From the human side, what is transferred to Christ is not our guilt so much as our nature. Athanasius thus almost combines the four events of Christ's birth, life, death, and resurrection.

The concept of deification

With good reason, Robert Letham writes of Athanasius: 'There are three basic axes to his theology—creation, incarnation, and deification.'[56] To Athanasius, the Word is 'the deifying and enlightening power of the Father'. Hence, 'even if God had judged it good not to create, he would nonetheless have had his Word'.[57] By partaking of Him, we partake of the Father, for only what is truly divine is capable of deifying.[58] Possibly about 356–360, Athanasius wrote: 'For therefore the union was of this kind, that he might unite what is man by nature to him who is

53. Athanasius, *Discourse Against the Arians* 2.55.

54. Athanasius, *Against the Gentiles* 1.

55. Athanasius, *To the Bishops of Africa* 7.

56. Robert Letham, *The Holy Trinity* (Phillipsburg, PA: P&R Publishing, 2004), p. 128.

57. Athanasius, *Discourse Against the Arians* 2.31.

58. Athanasius, *Councils of Ariminum and Seleucia* 51.

in the nature of the Godhead, and his salvation and deification might be sure.'[59] Athanasius affirmed both the true divinity of the Word from the Father against those whom he nicknamed 'Ariomaniacs',[60] and the true flesh from the ever-virgin Mary against the Gnostics.[61]

Athanasius's views have been critiqued by his critics on a number of grounds:

1. Athanasius fails to distinguish between Christ's humanity and ours.

2. His concept of divinization is mechanical or automatic.

3. He omits Christ's sacrificial death.

Jeffrey Finch writes of Athanasius, that he 'may not have integrated the atoning death of Christ on the cross with his doctrine of divinization as fully as he could have done'.[62] To Epictetus, the bishop of Corinth, Athanasius wrote: 'And truly it is strange that it was he who suffered and yet suffered not. Suffered, because his own body suffered, and he was in it, which thus suffered; suffered not, because the Word, being by nature God, is impassible.'[63] He anticipated Cyril, bishop of Alexandria from 412 to 444, in saying that 'he himself was harmed in no respect, as he is impassible and incorruptible and the very Word and God, but he cared for and saved suffering men, for whom he endured these things, by his impassibility'.[64]

---

59. Athanasius, *Discourse Against the Arians* 2.70.

60. The nickname may have come from Eustathius of Antioch who used it in a letter which may be dated before 328-329. See Alastair B. Logan, 'Marcellus of Ancyra' (Pseudo-Anthimus), 'On the Holy Church': Text, Translation and Commentary,' *Journal of Theological Studies* 51, no. 1 (2000): p. 104, n.8.

61. Athanasius, *Discourse Against the Arians* 2.70.

62. Jeffrey Finch, 'Athanasius on the Deifying Work of the Redeemer' in *Theosis: Deification in Christian Theology*, eds. Stephen Finlan and Vladimir Kharlamov (Eugene, OR: Pickwick Publications, 2006), pp. 115-116.

63. Athanasius, *Letter* 59.6.

64. Athanasius, *On the Incarnation* 54.

Regarding creation, Athanasius had no Gnostic or Manichaean tendencies. It was inexcusable for the pagans to worship that which was carved in stone, chipped out of wood, or painted as art.[65] The creation reveals the creator: 'For often the artist, even when not seen, is known by his works.'[66] The order of the universe shows that there is one creator, for a ship can only be steered by one, and a lyre can only be played by one; otherwise, there would be disorder and disharmony.[67]

For Athanasius, redemption meant incorruption, for, as noted above, the enemy was not so much sin but death. Hence the focus was on the incarnation and the resurrection rather than on the crucifixion and the atonement. In his third discourse against the Arians, Athanasius explained:

> For as, although there be one Son by nature, true and only-begotten, we too become sons, not as he in nature and truth, but according to the grace of him who calls, and though we are men from the earth, are yet called gods, not as the true God or his Word, but as has pleased God who has given us that grace.[68]

'Deification' meant to receive divine attributes such as everlasting life, as per John 3:16.

The humanity of Christ

Adolf von Harnack famously claimed of Athanasius that 'the man who saved the character of Christianity as a religion of living fellowship with God, was the man from whose Christology almost every trait which recalls the historical Jesus

---

65. Cf. Athanasius, *Against the Gentiles* 5–36.

66. Ibid., 35.

67. Ibid., 39.

68. Athanasius, *Against the Arians* 3.19. Athanasius refers to John 10:34 where Psalm 82:6 is cited. Scholarly opinion has generally rejected the authenticity of the fourth book of *Against the Arians*, but, despite Charles Kannengiesser's one-time qualms, has accepted the third book as authentic. See Ernest, *The Bible in Athanasius of Alexandria*, p. 111.

of Nazareth was erased'.[69] This has bite but is less than fair.[70] Formally, Athanasius was committed to the full humanity of Christ: 'although he is incorporeal by nature and Word, yet through the mercy and goodness of his Father he appeared to us in a human body for our salvation'.[71] In the flesh, Christ was hungry, thirsty, He slept, He labored, He wept, and, most vitally, He died.[72] Athanasius further comments: 'For if the Lord had not become man, we had not been redeemed from sin, not raised from the dead, but remaining dead under the earth; not exalted into heaven, but lying in Hades.'[73] He asserted that Christ assumed a body, 'and that not foreign to our own'.[74] It was 'a true, not an unreal, body'.[75] But in practice, Athanasius struggled to give that its full meaning because of his view that in the incarnation, the Son of God deified His own manhood. Athanasius attempted to hold together the incarnation of the Word and the immutability of the Word. Since Christ is both God and man, He was in the body, yet at the same time, He ordered the universe.[76] To quote Athanasius: 'The most amazing thing is this, that he both lived as a man, and as the Word gave life to everything, as the Son was with the Father'.[77] Christ was 'not bound to the body, but rather he controlled it, so he was in it and in everything, and outside creation'.[78] Divinity entered humanity while remaining totally divine. Christ was 'harmed in

69. Adolf von Harnack, *History of Dogma*, trans. Neil Buchanan (New York: Dover Publications, 1961), 4:45.

70. See Letham, *The Holy Trinity*, pp. 130-133 for his rejection of the view that Athanasius had no place for a human soul in Jesus.

71. Athanasius, *On the Incarnation* 1.

72. David Brakke, *Athanasius and Asceticism* (London: The John Hopkins University Press, 1998), p. 287.

73. Athanasius, *Discourse Against the Arians* 1.43.

74. Athanasius, *On the Incarnation* 8.

75. Ibid., 18.

76. Ibid., 18.

77. Ibid., 17.

78. Ibid., 17.

no respect, as he is impassible and incorruptible and the very Word and God'.[79] In short, 'as he is in creation, yet in no way partakes of creation, but rather everything partakes of his power, so also, although he used the body as an instrument, he partook of none of the body's attributes, but rather himself sanctified the body'.[80] Indeed, 'neither when the Virgin gave birth did he suffer himself nor when he was in the body was he polluted, but rather he sanctified the body', as the sun is not destroyed by terrestrial bodies or darkness but illuminates them.[81]

Athanasius thus emphasised not the humiliation of the incarnation (as in Phil. 2:5-11), but the retention of the divine attributes. The one who was in the form of God took on the form of a servant, but the key point is not the humiliation of the Word but the exaltation of the servant. The Word could not be exalted because the Word is already exalted. It was the humanity which is exalted due to the Word's obedience. It is not that Athanasius did not believe that Jesus is the suffering servant of Isaiah, but that such a portrayal of the Word does not easily fit into his understanding of the work of Christ.

Most powerfully, in his *Easter Letter* from 338, Athanasius summed up the mission of the Lord:

> For he suffered to prepare freedom from suffering for those who suffer in him. He descended that he might raise us up, he took on himself the trial of being born, that we might love him who is unbegotten, he went down to corruption, that corruption might put on immortality, he became weak for us, that we might rise with power, he descended to death, that we who die as men might live again, and that death should no more reign over us, for the Apostolic word proclaims, 'Death shall not have the dominion over us.'[82]

---

79.   Ibid., 54.

80.   Ibid., 43.

81.   Ibid., 17.

82.   Athanasius, *Easter Letter* 10.8.

Biblical balance and a judicious use of paradox made for a compelling presentation of the work of the Son of God.

J. N. D. Kelly has interpreted Athanasius's Christology in terms of the Word-flesh scheme.[83] Such a Christology distinguished Word from flesh, prompting Athanasius to write that 'the Word was not able to die, being immortal and the Son of the Father—therefore he took to himself a body which could die'.[84] This needs to be heavily qualified as G. D. Dragas has shown how often Athanasius would use 'flesh' (*sarx*) as a synonym for 'man' (*anthropos*) or 'body' (*sōma*).[85] This did not keep Athanasius from getting into difficulties as he tried to explain Christ's humanity, and it must be said that there are unsatisfactory aspects to his treatment of Jesus's suffering and death. Christ's humanity is in danger of being swallowed up into His divinity. Athanasius asked: 'Did he not hunger then?' and he then proceeded to answer: 'Yes, he hungered because of the body's nature. But he did not die of starvation because the Lord was wearing that body.'[86] There is a genuine tension here. The Bible presents Christ as having complete control over His death and resurrection (e.g., John 10:17-18), yet also describes His genuine agony in the Garden of Gethsemane (Matt.26:36-46).

To Athanasius, the deeds of Christ on earth were more divine than human. Athanasius struggled with Jesus's hunger, thirst, sleep, suffering, and death, and instead pointed to all the miracles. He wrote: 'The fact that he commanded demons and cast them out was not a human deed, but a divine one. Or who, seeing him healing the diseases to which the race of men was subject, would still think that he was a man and not God?'[87] Jesus's miracles are proof that He is Lord of creation. In

---

83.   Kelly, *Early Christian Doctrines*, p. 287.

84   Athanasius, *On the Incarnation* 9.

85.   J. Leemans, 'Thirteen Years of Athanasius Research (1985-1998): A Survey and Bibliography,' *Sacris Erudiri* 39 (2000): p. 181.

86.   Athanasius, *On the Incarnation* 21.

87.   Ibid., 18.

Athanasius's estimation of Christ: 'His works are not human but superhuman'.[88]

All these considerations come to the fore in Athanasius's debate with the Arians. The Arians had pointed to biblical texts that spoke of Christ's troubled soul, His desire to avoid crucifixion, His growth in wisdom and stature, His destitution on the cross, and His ignorance of the date of the last day.[89] The apostle declared of Christ: In Him 'are hidden all the treasures of wisdom and knowledge' (Col. 2:3), yet Christ Himself had said with regard to His second coming: 'But concerning that day or that hour, no one knows, not even the angels in heaven, nor the Son, but only the Father' (Mark 13:32; the 'only' is actually added from the parallel passage in Matt. 24:36). Basil of Caesarea tried to argue that Jesus meant that 'of that day no one knows, neither the angels nor the Son if not for the Father'.[90] Augustine of Hippo argued that Jesus meant that He would not reveal the day or hour ('to know' can be understood as 'to reveal' in Gen. 22:12 and Deut. 13:3).[91]

In Athanasius's view, Christ's anguish and ignorance were, to some degree, feigned. The Son knows the Father and so knows the day of judgment, and 'he, who speaks of the antecedents of the day, knows certainly the day also'.[92] There could be no real ignorance in Christ (see John 6:6; 11:14): 'the flesh indeed is ignorant, but the Word himself, considered as the Word, knows all things even before they come to be'.[93] This may not

88. Ibid., 48.

89. Athanasius, *Against the Arians* 3. 26–27.

90. See Francis X. Gumerlock, 'Mark 13:32 and Christ's Supposed Ignorance: Four Patristic Solutions,' *Trinity Journal* 28 (2007): pp. 206–207.

91. See Gumerlock, 'Mark 13:32 and Christ's Supposed Ignorance,' pp. 207–208. Also Michael Cameron, *Christ Meets Me Everywhere: Augustine's Early Figurative Exegesis*, Oxford Studies in Historical Theology (Oxford: Oxford University Press, 2012), p. 174; Saint Augustine, *Expositions of the Psalms*, vol. 1. 1–32, trans. Maria Boulding (Hyde Park, NY: New City Press, 2000), pp. 104, 158.

92. Athanasius, *Four Discourses Against the Arians* 3.42.

93. Ibid., 3.38.

be identified with Augustine's later interpretation, because Athanasius considered that the Word as God knew the day and hour while the man as flesh did not. Hence, 'it is plain that he knows also the hour of the end of all things, as the Word, though as man he is ignorant of it, for ignorance is proper to man'.[94] He could say that Christ as man weeps (John 11:35), but as God, He raises Lazarus from the dead (John 11:43-44). Also, Christ 'used to hunger and thirst physically, while divinely he fed five thousand persons from five loaves'.[95] Some things are said of His humanity and some of His deity.[96] In Athanasius's portrayal of Christ, the flesh suffered, but not the Word which had taken this flesh. Athanasius concluded:

> Wherefore of necessity when he was in a body suffering, and weeping, and toiling, these things, which are proper to the flesh, are ascribed to him together with the body. If then he wept and was troubled, it was not the Word, considered as the Word, who wept and was troubled, but it was proper to the flesh; and if too he besought that the cup might pass away, it was not the Godhead that was in terror, but this affection too was proper to the manhood.[97]

The divine Word remained immutable and impassible (note Heb. 13:8), while the flesh was subject to weakness and suffering.

As a result, Christ bore His sufferings only as though they were His own. To use Athanasius's words: 'The Word bore the infirmities of the flesh, as his own, for his was the flesh; and the flesh ministered to the works of the Godhead, because the Godhead was in it, for the body was God's'.[98] He did point out that 'when the flesh suffered, the Word was not external

---

94. Athanasius, *Against the Arians* 3.43.

95. Athanasius, *On the Opinion of Dionysius* 9.

96. Ibid., 10.

97. Athanasius, *Against the Arians* 3.56.

98. Ibid., 3.31.

to it',[99] but he refused to consider that the Word qua Word could suffer. There is no doubt that he would have agreed with Cyril of Alexandria that Christ, 'though being by his own nature impassible, suffered in the flesh for us, according to the Scriptures, and he was in the crucified flesh impassibly making his own the sufferings of his own flesh'.[100]

The deification of the Son's humanity, before the resurrection and ascension, seems to be a difficulty in Athanasius's view of Christ. He wrote: 'For he did not, when he became man, cease to be God; nor, whereas he is God does he shrink from what is man's—perish the thought—but rather, being God, he has taken to him the flesh, and being in the flesh deifies the flesh.'[101] If the fullness of this process could be found in the incarnation, then the child in Mary's womb would have known the date of the second coming. Athanasius groped towards an answer for this problem when he accepted that Christ advanced in the body and in the manifestation of the Godhead.[102] Later in his ministry, he seems to have been more at ease with the full humanity of Christ: 'For he was made man, as it is written, and it belongs to men to be ignorant, as it belongs to them to hunger and the rest.'[103]

In combining the Word's incarnation with His immutability, Athanasius confronted problems in coming to a satisfactory view of the sufferings of Christ. Related to this is the question of whether Athanasius envisaged Christ's humanity as including a human rational soul or whether he regarded the Word as taking the place of one. J. N. D. Kelly considers that Athanasius's

99. Ibid., 3.32.

100. In E. R. Hardy, ed., *Christology of the Later Fathers* (Philadelphia, PA: Westminster Press, 1954), p. 351. See also Paul L. Gavrilyuk, *The Suffering of the Impassible God* (Oxford: Oxford University Press, 2006).

101. Athanasius *Four Discourses Against the Arians* 3.38.

102. Ibid., 3.52.

103. Athanasius *Concerning the Holy Spirit* Letter 2.9.

thought 'simply allowed no room for a human mind'.[104] Aloys Grillmeier also concludes that Athanasius viewed Christ as 'nothing else but a visible body and the invisible Word'.[105] If indeed, Athanasius did consider that Christ was only the Word plus flesh (sarx), then his Christology runs counter to the orthodox tradition, which has always maintained, in the well-known phrase of Gregory of Nazianzus, that 'what is not assumed is not healed'.[106] Redemption of the human soul is thus not possible unless Christ possessed a human soul. Certainly, in his discussion of Christ's anguish in the Garden and on the cross and His ignorance of the last day, Athanasius did not point to the limitations of Christ's human soul.

It is fundamental to Athanasius's Christology that the Word 'did not become other than himself on taking the flesh, but, being the same as before, he was robed in it'.[107] Yet, for all this, Athanasius had no wish to fuse the humanity of Christ into the Godhead, so he asked, rather indelicately: 'What Hades has emitted the statement that the body of Mary is *homoousios* with the Godhead of the Word?'[108] In a letter to Epictetus, he wrote: 'By the very fact that the Saviour became man really and truly, the whole man was saved.'[109] Christ had 'a true, not an unreal, body'.[110] In fact, the Word of God even spat.[111] In his formal statements, the fiery Athanasius completely rejected Docetism, and also, to be a little anachronistic, Apollinarianism and Monophysitism. The incarnation was a true one: 'He became man, and did not come into man.'[112]

---

104. Kelly, *Early Christian Doctrine*, p. 287.

105. Aloys Grillmeier, *Christ in Christian Tradition* (London: Mowbrays, 1975), 1:317.

106. Gregory of Nazianzus, *Epistle 51*.

107. Athanasius, *Against the Arians* 2.8.

108. Athanasius, *Epistle 59.2*.

109. Cited in G. S. Hendry, *The Gospel of the Incarnation* (London: SCM, 1959), p. 48, n.8.

110. Athanasius, *On the Incarnation* 18.

111. Athanasius, *Against the Arians* 3.41.

112. Ibid., 3. 30.

Grillmeier rightly observes that Athanasius's Christological thought 'veers from *becoming flesh* to *dwelling in the flesh* as in a temple'.[113] Thus, Athanasius made many statements about the Word dwelling in the body.[114] Athanasius hovered right on the border of what later became known as Apollinarianism, and it may be that only after the synod of Alexandria in 362 was he able to appreciate more fully the doctrine that Christ assumed a body with intelligence. Athanasius believed in the human soul of Christ, but, because of the nature of the controversy in which he was embroiled, naturally laid a disproportionate emphasis on the deity of the Word.

The resurrection of Christ

In Athanasius's scheme of salvation, the Word defeated sin and paid its dreadful penalty, but the major emphasis was on the defeat of death. He wrote:

> Since the Word realized that the corruption of men would not be abolished in any other way except by everyone dying—but the Word was not able to die, being immortal and the Son of the Father—therefore he took to himself a body which could die, in order that, since this participated in the Word who is above all, it might suffice for death on behalf of all, and because of the Word who was dwelling in it, it might remain incorruptible, and so corruption might cease from all men by the grace of the resurrection.[115]

Christ did fulfil the debt by His death where 'he offered to death the body which he had taken to himself'.[116] Nevertheless, the result was more in terms of immortality than acquittal: 'The incorruptible Son of God was united to all men by his body similar to theirs' and so 'he endued all men with incorruption'.[117]

113. Grillmeier, *Christ in Christian Tradition*, 1:327.

114. Athanasius, *On the Incarnation* 9, 20.

115. Ibid., 9.

116. Ibid., 9.

117. Ibid., 9.

Athanasius's illustration is very revealing:

> As when a great king has entered some great city and dwelt in
> one of the houses in it, such a city is then greatly honoured,
> and no longer does any enemy or bandit come against it, but it
> is rather treated with regard because of the king who has taken
> up residence in one of its houses; so also is the case with the
> King of all.[118]

Christ is not so much the sacrificed lamb as the victorious lion:
'since by men death had laid hold of men, so for this reason by
the incarnation of God the Word were effected the overthrow
of death and the resurrection of life'.[119] Christ overcame sin
and death, but the emphasis falls on the latter. Athanasius
wrote:

> No one else could bring what was corrupted to incorruptibility,
> except the Saviour himself, who also created the universe in the
> beginning from nothing; nor could any other recreate men in
> the image, save the image of the Father; nor could another raise
> up what was mortal as immortal, save our Lord Jesus Christ,
> who is life itself.[120]

Christ paid the debt, which had to be paid—it was a real
death.[121] Therefore, the Word's body was 'mortal and died
in the fashion of those similar to it'.[122] The body was both
similar and dissimilar to ours, as Athanasius explained:
'Through the coming of the Word into it, it was no longer
corruptible according to its nature, but because of the Word
who was dwelling in it, it became immune from corruption.'[123]
Athanasius thus added:

---

118. Ibid., 9.
119. Ibid., 10.
120. Ibid., 20.
121. Ibid., 20.
122. Ibid., 20.
123. Ibid., 20.

> The trophy of his victory over death was the showing of the resurrection to all, and their assurance that he had erased corruption and hence that their bodies would be incorruptible; and as a pledge and proof of the resurrection which all would enjoy he kept his own body incorruptible.[124]

Hence Jesus suffered from the consequences of the Fall, but not from any diseases.

The use of paradox

To explain Christ's death, Athanasius resorted to heavy doses of paradox and this had implications for how he treated the deaths of believers. He wrote of the Lord's body: 'It was unable not to die, as it was mortal and had been offered to death on behalf of all, for which very reason the Saviour had prepared it for himself; but it was also unable to remain dead, because it had become the temple of life.'[125] 'Therefore it died as being mortal, but came to life because of the life which was in it.'[126]

The Saviour suffers, but mainly triumphs, and this is passed onto His people. Athanasius thus declared that all Christians tread on death 'as something non-existent'.[127] Hence the Christian martyrs facing death are portrayed as those who trample a serpent underfoot or as children making sport of a lion.[128] So, in Athanasius's view, two things occurred simultaneously: 'The death of all was fulfilled in the Lord's body, and also death and corruption were destroyed because of the Word who was in it'[129]

Like Cyril, Athanasius had to resort to paradox, claiming:

> The things which the human body of the Word suffered, the Word, being one with it, transferred to himself, in order that we

124. Ibid., 22.
125. Ibid., 31.
126. Ibid., 31.
127. Ibid., 27.
128. Ibid., 29.
129. Ibid., 20.

might be enabled to become partakers of the divine nature of the Word. And it was a paradox, that he was a sufferer and not a sufferer—a sufferer because his own body suffered and he was in it as it suffered; and not a sufferer because the Word, being by nature God, cannot suffer.[130]

In the same vein, he wrote of the Lord's body: 'It was unable not to die, as it was mortal and had been offered to death on behalf of all, for which very reason the Saviour had prepared it for himself; but it was also unable to remain dead, because it had become the temple of life.'[131] Therefore, Athanasius argued, 'it died as being mortal, but came to life because of the life which was in it'.[132] But when does a paradox like this become a contradiction?

A paradox is necessary in order to maintain the biblical faith, as Charles Wesley realised when he wrote the words:

Amazing love! how can it be
That thou, my God, shouldst die for me?
'Tis mystery all! The Immortal dies:
Who can explore his strange design? ...

'Tis mercy all! let earth adore,
Let angel minds inquire no more.

Similarly, Stuart Townend's modern hymn, *In Christ Alone*, has the line: 'Fullness of God in helpless babe'.

Any discussion of God will invariably be analogical and even paradoxical, but Athanasius's talk of impassible suffering does strain credibility, for there is something of an air of unreality about his account of the sufferings of Christ. In the 1940s Dietrich Bonhoeffer sought to correct this by asserting that the 'The Bible directs man to God's powerlessness and suffering;

---

130. Cited in Reinhold Seeberg, *Text-Book of the History of Doctrines* (Grand Rapids, MI: Baker, 1964), p. 212.

131. Athanasius, *On the Incarnation* 31.

132. Ibid., 31.

only the suffering God can help.'[133] While such a statement cannot be said to be true to the whole biblical revelation, Bonhoeffer was trying to take the sufferings of Christ with complete seriousness. Before one is too hard on Athanasius's paradoxes, one should cite Bonhoeffer's: 'The God who lets us live in the world without the working hypothesis of God is the God before whom we stand continually. Before God and with God we live without God.'[134] It was not only the great Alexandrian bishop who struggled to understand how the infinite, holy and all-knowing God descends to finite, corrupt, and ignorant human beings.

A summary

Whatever his defects, Athanasius took seriously the deity of Christ and His immutability. As a result, he claimed that almost before His birth, the Word was reigning and despoiling His enemies.[135] An outlook such as this makes it difficult to deal with the sufferings and death of Christ. One could even question whether the sufferings and the death were in any sense real. The problem is inherent in any attempt to define the nature and person of the God-man. The mystery lies within the New Testament itself and the Council of Chalcedon was wise not to press it too closely. Nonetheless, Athanasius may have ventured to have been a little more daring in his treatment of the suffering and ignorance of Christ. The great bishop's paradoxes belie an unwillingness to some degree to take the world and hence the incarnation with the seriousness that they deserve. He could do no other, given the deification principle, which formed the basis of his soteriology. Orthodoxy is left to wrestle with the question: 'Can God remain God and yet be mutable and passible?' In the end, however, Reinhold Seeberg is right to

133. Dietrich Bonhoeffer, *Letters and Papers from Prison* (London: SCM, 1971), p. 361.

134. Ibid., p. 360.

135. Athanasius, *On the Incarnation* p. 36.

point out the affinities which Athanasius's Christology has with the New Testament Christologies of Paul and John, and to conclude that Athanasius's Christology is a genuinely Christian one, however one-sided its interpretation might be in certain places.[136]

136. Seeberg, *History of Doctrines*, p. 214.

...

7

'A MAN IN CHRIST':

*Athanasius's View of the Bible, Asceticism
and Spirituality*

'Keep your heart with all vigilance, for from it flow the springs of life,' says Proverbs 4:23. It is well worth our seeking to take stock of what drove Athanasius to write as he did, to stand firm as he did, and to testify to the person of Jesus Christ as he did, both inside and outside the professing church. It is natural, therefore, to glean what we can of Athansius's view of the Bible, his ascetic ideals, and his general spiritual outlook.

Athanasius and the Bible
Earlier, we noted Athanasius's love of the Psalms, and his drawing on them to fortify himself in all his troubles. He also drew on the Apocrypha, notably the Wisdom of Solomon and Baruch, and at times seems to have regarded them as part of the Old Testament. Esther, however, was omitted, although he cites it in his *Easter Letter* of 338.[1] As a bishop, he must have preached hundreds, even thousands, of times, but precious little of this has come down to us; what he preached on a Sunday morning is, as Peter Leithart says, 'largely irrecoverable'.[2] Moreover, he never wrote a commentary on a biblical book.

---

1.   James D. Ernest, *The Bible in Athanasius of Alexandria*, The Bible in Ancient
      Christianity 2 (Leiden: Brill, 2004), 83; Athanasius, *Easter Letter* 10.11.

2.   Peter Leithart, *Athanasius* (Grand Rapids, MI: Baker, 2011), p. 29.

Nevertheless, Athanasius's biblical mind-set is obvious to all, and his view of the authority of the Bible can be gleaned from his extant writings. For example, Athanasius's *Easter Letter* of 367 lists the twenty-seven canonical books of the New Testament. Referring to these, he declared:

> These are fountains of salvation, that they who thirst may be satisfied with the living words they contain. In these alone is proclaimed the doctrine of godliness. Let no man add to these, neither let him take aught from these.

It was an important statement on the authority and sufficiency of Scripture. Indeed, Athanasius had declared that the Scriptures are sufficient to declare the truth right back at the beginning of his *Against the Gentiles*.[3] He was to tell the monks: 'The Scriptures are sufficient for instruction.'[4] It was a message often repeated. About Easter 356, during exile in the desert, he wrote to the bishops of Egypt: 'Holy Scripture is of all things most sufficient for us'.[5] It was a message he repeated after the Councils of Ariminum and Seleucia in 359: 'Divine Scripture is sufficient above all things'.[6] As God had warned Moses about neither adding to nor subtracting from the divine revelation (Deut. 12:32), so Athanasius too formally held to a Bible-only creed[7]—wine and water were not to be mixed.

In 347, responding to those who played off the prophets' emphasis on moral over ceremonial law (e.g. Isa. 1:12; Jer. 7:22) in order to draw the conclusion that the Scriptures contradict themselves—prefiguring liberal theology—Athanasius would have none of it. God is truth and so cannot lie (Heb. 6:18), and He had appointed the sacrifices as shadows of the good things to

3. Athanasius, *Against the Gentiles* 1.

4. Athanasius, *The Life of Antony* 16.

5. Athanasius, *To the Bishops of Egypt* 4.

6. Athanasius, *Councils of Ariminum and Seleucia* 6.

7. David Brakke, *Athanasius and Asceticism* (London: The John Hopkins University Press, 1998), p. 330.

come (Heb. 10:1; 9:10).[8] The Bible was not viewed as a collection of contradictory documents. Rather, it forms a coherent whole, indicating the divine mind behind it. Gregory of Nazianzus stated that Athanasius had meditated on every book of the Old and New Testament.[9] Alas, we have so few insights into his life as a preacher, but he must have been effective. One finds nuggets of gold in his writings, as when he compared the Garden of Eden and Golgotha: 'There the taste was sweet, but the act was bitter; here, however, the food was bitter, but the result was sweet.'[10] He believed most firmly that 'the Lord is present in the words of the Scriptures'.[11]

These convictions, however, did not keep him from somewhat odd applications. So, for example, he wrote of Christ: 'Neither did he undergo the death of John by being beheaded, nor like Isaiah was he sawn asunder, in order that he might keep his body intact and whole in death and that there be no pretext for those who wish to divide the Church'.[12] He also considered that by dying on the cross Jesus died in the air. Hence He purified the air from demons, and so opened the way up to heaven.[13] He spiritualized the exhortation to imitate the diligence of the ant in Proverbs 6:6-8, and interpreted it to mean that we ought to be watchful over our souls, as Mark 14:37 exhorts.[14] Because he often cited from memory, he occasionally tripped up, as when he inadvertently changed Jesus's reference to 'the power of God' and 'the Scriptures' to the 'power of the Scriptures' (Matt. 22:29).[15]

---

8.   Athanasius, *Easter Letter* 19.3-4 (for 347).

9.   Gregory of Nazianzus, *Oration* 21 (NPNF2 7:6).

10. Brakke, *Athanasius and Asceticism*, p. 293.

11. Cited in Ernest, *The Bible in Athanasius of Alexandria*, p. 336.

12. Athanasius, *On the Incarnation* 24

13. Ibid., 25. There are variants here in the recensions. Cf. F. L. Cross, *The Study of St Athanasius* (Oxford: Clarendon Press, 1945), pp. 12-13.

14. Brakke, *Athanasius and Asceticism*, pp. 87, 89.

15. Cited in Ernest, *The Bible in Athanasius of Alexandria*, p. 27.

To testify to the deity of Christ, he appealed to a number of texts, especially in the Gospel of John (e.g. John 1:1, 3, 14; 10:30; 14:9-10),[16] and to appeal to Constantius, he adopted the stance of the apostle Paul (e.g. Acts 24:10; 26:25-26; 2 Cor. 1:23).[17] To the monk, Amoun, he urged that the monks be taught Scripture, as the Psalmist had prayed: 'Give me life, O Lord, according to your word!' (Ps. 119:107).[18] Again, he emphasized that Christ alone is the true teacher, and He teaches through His written word within the one church, which therefore is under divine obligation to teach that same word. Athanasius was not in John Bunyan's league, but his blood was bibline.

Asceticism and the Monastic Movement

The fourth century was a strange new age for the church—she had a taste of worldly power and witnessed a flowering of unworldly asceticism. Around the year 360, or perhaps a year or two earlier, Athanasius wrote his extraordinarily popular *Life of Antony*. Indeed, Arnaldo Momigliano calls it 'one of the most influential books of any time',[19] while Robert C. Gregg says it was 'an immediate literary sensation'.[20] In the fourth century, it was probably more popular and better known than his *On the Incarnation of the Word*. There seems little reason to follow H. M. Gwatkin who did not regard it as coming from Athanasius and that Antony never existed![21] Timothy Barnes and L. W. Barnard are two of a number of more modern historians who

---

16. Ibid., pp. 154-155.

17. Ibid., pp. 224-226.

18. L. W. Barnard, trans., *The Monastic Letters of Saint Athanasius the Great* (Oxford: SLG Press, 2002), p. 3.

19. Arnaldo Momigliano, 'Introduction: Christianity and the Decline of the Roman Empire' in *The Conflict Between Paganism and Christianity in the Fourth Century*, ed. Arnaldo Momigliano (Oxford: Clarendon Press, 1963), p. 11.

20. Athanasius, *The Life of Antony and the Letter to Marcellinus*, trans. Robert C. Gregg (New York: Paulist Press, 1980), p. 2.

21. H. M. Gwatkin, *The Arian Controversy* (1908 ed.; repr Eugene, OR: Wipf and Stock, 2001), p. 48.

also believe, without sufficient reason, that the biography is not by Athanasius.[22] More recently, David Gwynn has accepted its authenticity.[23]

Athanasius seems to have known Antony personally, as the bishop says, rather elusively, that he followed Antony 'more than a few times' and that he 'poured water over his hands' (see 2 Kings 3:11).[24] Athanasius had strong links with the monks and made good use of these connections when he was hiding in the desert. In his *Life of Antony*, Athanasius records that when Antony was leaving the city, 'we' were setting him on his way, and 'we' arrived at the gate. If the *we*-passages in Acts indicate the presence of Luke with Paul, so too this *we*-passage in *Antony* indicates Athanasius's presence with Antony.[25] That Athanasius had good political reason to write Antony's biography is not to be doubted—the support of the monks in Egypt was very significant—but Athanasius had already gained that support and his admiration for Antony was deep and genuine.

The fourth century was an age when monks had tended to be suspicious of clerics, as akin to compromising with the world, but Athanasius encouraged monks to become bishops. Pachomius had feared ordination, and later Ammonius, one of the Tall Brothers, threatened to cut off his left ear to avoid the dreaded ceremony, and should that not prove enough, threatened to cut out his own tongue.[26] Antony, said Athanasius, 'honored the rule of the Church with extreme care, and he wanted every cleric to be held in higher regard than himself. He felt not shame at

22. T. D. Barnes, *Athanasius and Constantius* (Cambridge, MA: Harvard University Press, 1993), p. 240, n.64. See also J. Leemans, 'Thirteen Years of Athanasius Research (1985-1998): A Survey and Bibliography,' *Sacris Erudiri* 39 (2000): pp. 156, 158.

23. David Gwynn, *Athanasius of Alexandria: Bishop, Theologian, Ascetic, Father, Christian Theology in Context* (Oxford: Oxford University Press, 2012), p. 15.

24. Athanasius, *The Life of Antony*, Introduction.

25. Ibid., 71. For the 'we' passages in Acts, see, for example, Acts 16:11-16; 20:6, 7, 13; 21:1-17.

26. See Brakke, *Athanasius and Asceticism*, p. 109.

bowing the head to the bishops and priests.'[27] Just before his conversion in 386, the great Augustine of Hippo seems to have known nothing of the monastic movement, despite the fact that there was a monastery in Milan where he was living. This only changed when a fellow North African Ponticianus told Augustine and his close friend Alypius of Antony, the renowned Egyptian monk.[28] Evagrius of Antioch had translated Athanasius's *Life of Antony* into Latin about 370 and there was another, anonymous, translation that had appeared before then. In turmoil of soul, Augustine turned to Alypius and said of the monks: 'What is the matter with us? What is the meaning of this story? These men have not had our schooling, yet they stand up and storm the gates of heaven while we, for all our learning, lie here, grovelling in this world of flesh and blood!'[29]

Athanasius himself was an ascetic, and Jeffrey Finch is prepared to venture the criticism that his practices were 'possibly still tainted with a certain measure of Hellenistic spirit-matter dualism'.[30] This is undoubtedly true, but the bishop could still write sometime before 354 that 'All things made by God are beautiful and pure, for the Word of God has made nothing useless or impure.'[31] Compared to some others, Athanasius was fairly moderate in his asceticism, but he appreciated Antony's battles with demons who came to him in various forms, notably as women, young boys, wild beasts, or soldiers. Antony repressed his body and passed many a night without sleep.[32] He would eat bread and salt, often ate only once a day, or even once every

27. Athanasius, *The Life of Antony*, trans. Gregg, p. 67.

28. Augustine, *Confessions* 8.6.

29. Ibid., 8.8.

30. Jeffrey Finch, 'Athanasius on the Deifying Work of the Redeemer' in *Theosis: Deification in Christian Theology*, eds. Stephen Finlan and Vladimir Kharlamov (Eugene, OR: Pickwick Publications, 2006), p. 113.

31. Athanasius, *Letter 48*.

32. Athanasius, *The Life of Antony*, trans. Gregg, p. 7. Elsewhere, Athanasius did defend a 'natural use' for sleep (Brakke, *Athanasius and Asceticism*, 312).

second or fourth day,[33] and did not bathe, not even washing his feet.[34] He would weave baskets to give to visitors in return for what they brought him.[35]

Athanasius believed that Antony performed miracles,[36] but did not believe that all who came to him were healed.[37] When a military officer came to Antony to ask him to pray for his demon-disturbed daughter, Antony replied: 'Why do you cry out to me, man? I too am a man like you, but if you believe in Christ, whom I serve, go, and in the same way you believe, pray to God, and it will come to pass.'[38] Athanasius also came to criticise those who exhumed the bones of martyrs, and instead urged them to 'confess him whom the martyrs confess'.[39] Noting Matthew 7:21 and Luke 10:20, Athanasius pointed out that the working of signs is the Savior's work, not ours, and, in any case, virtue counts for more than signs.[40] He viewed Antony as being in 'utter equilibrium', living by reason, not ruled by passions.[41] To Athanasius, Antony was the picture of a Christian: he was 'never troubled, his soul being calm, and he never looked gloomy, his mind being joyous'.[42] His lifestyle does not seem to have harmed him and when he came to die aged 105, Antony apparently still possessed his eyesight and all his teeth![43]

The monastic world tended to be a platonic world, which could become a haven for Gnosticism. Extremism and

---

33. Ibid., p. 7.
34. Ibid., p. 47.
35. Ibid., p. 53.
36. Ibid., pp. 14, 15, 48, 57, 58, 61.
37. Ibid., p. 56.
38. Ibid., p. 48.
39. See Carl Beckwith, 'Athanasius' in *Shapers of Christian Orthodoxy*, ed. Bradley G. Green (Nottingham: Apollos, 2010), p 181.
40. Athanasius, *The Life of Antony*, trans. Gregg, p. 38.
41. Ibid., p. 14.
42. Ibid., p. 67.
43. Ibid., p. 93.

insight competed in the mind and soul of Athanasius. From John 19:26-27, Athanasius argued that Mary had no other children and so was perpetually a virgin, and from Luke 1:28-30 he claimed that she was not familiar with the male voice.[44] There are rewards in the heavenly kingdom (Luke 19:16-19; Matt.13:1-23), and Athanasius connected these with ascetic practices, but he responded vigorously to an extremist like Hieracas who argued that Christ has rendered marriage an evil institution.[45] Athanasius linked the virgin to the one who was set over ten cities and the married woman to the one set over five (Luke 19:16-19), and understood the sixty-fold fruitfulness to apply to the married state and the hundred-fold to ascetics (Matt. 13:23). Yet he also pointed out that sixty is not evil because a hundred is greater, and marriage is portrayed as good in John 2:1-11, 1 Corinthians 7:5, and 1 Timothy 4:3 and 5:14.[46] To reject this, as Hieracas did, was to be guilty of 'great impiety' and 'hypocrisy'.[47]

To a monk, Ammoun, who struggled with involuntary sexual temptations at night, Athanasius affirmed the goodness of creation, and explained that sin flowed from our evil hearts, not dreams while we are asleep (Matt. 15:11). With some reserve, he spoke of sexual relations: 'Happy is the one who freely and naturally begets children in his youth.'[48] To another monk, Dracontius, who fled in order to escape ordination as a bishop, Athanasius wrote quite a vigorous letter, urging him to fulfil his duties to others.[49] Athanasius loved monasticism, but it was not the whole story—it was not given to every Christian to flee the world as some had done. He was relentless in his opposition to the 'super-spiritual' types who were involved in 'spiritual

44. Brakke, *Athanasius and Asceticism*, pp. 277, 279. This comes from Athanasius' First Letter to Virgins, in Coptic, and not regarded as authentic by all scholars.

45. Epiphanius, *Panarion* 67.

46. Brakke, *Athanasius and Asceticism*, pp. 282–283.

47. Ibid., 283.

48. Barnard, trans., *Monastic Letters*, p. 2.

49. Ibid., pp. 4–9.

marriages,' whereby celibates lived together without any sexual activity.[50] Pilgrimages to the Holy Land by virgins, some of whom lived at home with their parents and others who lived in communities, were treated as possibly beneficial, but there is an ambivalence about his attitude to them. Jerusalem was part of the shadow; Christ is the reality.[51]

As he was helping to shape the persecuted Confessing Church community at Finkenwalde Seminary in 1935, Dietrich Bonhoeffer wrote to his older brother Karl-Friedrich, 'The restoration of the church will surely come from a sort of new monasticism which has in common with the old only the uncompromising attitude of a life lived according to the Sermon on the Mount in the following of Christ. I believe it is now time to call people to this.'[52] Later, in his *Ethics*, he denounced 'two disastrous misunderstandings: the secular Protestant one and the monastic one'. He urged a return to the biblical and Reformational view of God's earthly calling (e.g. 1 Cor. 7:20) which includes radical obedience to Jesus Christ.[53] Christians are to be against the world in order to serve the world rightly. As a Protestant-turned-Catholic-turned-sceptic, the eighteenth-century author Edward Gibbon wrote, famously and fiercely, that:

> the monk, contracting the vices of a slave, devoutly followed the faith and passion of his ecclesiastical tyrant. The peace of the eastern church was invaded by a swarm of fanatics, incapable of fear, or reason, or humanity; and the Imperial troops acknowledged, without shame, that they were much less apprehensive of an encounter with the fiercest Barbarians.[54]

---

50. Cf. Brakke, *Athanasius and Asceticism*, p. 34.

51. Ibid., pp. 38-39.

52. Cited in William, Samson, 'The Finkenwalde Project' in *Monasticism Old and New* in Robert B. Kruschwtz, ed., *Christian Reflection: A Series in Faith and Ethics* (Waco, TX: Baylor University, 2010), p. 19.

53. Dietrich Bonhoeffer, *Ethics*, ed. Eberhard Bethge (London: SCM, 1963), pp. 223-225 (quotation from page 223).

54. E. Gibbon, *The History of the Decline and Fall of the Roman Empire*, ed. David Womersley (London: Penguin, 1995), 2:419.

One might say that the world came to be rescued from those who fled from it. There is surely some exaggeration here, along the lines of Rufinus who says that by the late fourth century, 'the multitude of monks in the deserts equals the population of the cities'.[55]

The Catholic and Orthodox position is put by Derwas Chitty and David Knowles, the latter portraying monasticism as essentially Christian, indeed as fulfilling the Beatitudes.[56] In Peter Brown's view, the holy man was often a mediator and arbiter—'a charismatic Ombudsman in a tension-ridden countryside'.[57] In the words of the distinguished Roman Catholic historian Christopher Dawson: 'Egyptian monasticism was the supreme achievement of oriental Christianity, and it expresses all that is best and worst in the national temperament.'[58] Monasticism deserves neither to be embraced nor summarily dismissed. Bonhoeffer's insights have much to commend them. The illiterates preserved literacy. Those seeking a passionless ideal could arouse fanaticism. And the attempt to be unworldly often led to an unbiblical dualism. Athanasius walked a tightrope, and he did not always retain a biblical balance, but he sought to be both in the world, yet not of the world.

The Spirituality of Athanasius

To Athanasius, the Christian life consisted of many things, but most important were knowing Scripture, engaging in prayer, living in a disciplined way, and providing for the poor. The life of faith was in harmony with reason, but we need to be aware of our limitations. Hence, he mocked those who asked, 'How can

---

55. Cited in C. Wilfred Griggs, *Early Egyptian Christianity from its Origins to 451 C.E.* (Leiden: Brill, 1988), p. 150.

56. David Knowles, *Christian Monasticism* (London: World University Library, 1969), p. 181.

57. Peter Brown, 'The Rise and Function of the Holy Man in Late Antiquity,' *Journal of Roman Studies* 61 (1971): p. 91.

58. Christopher Dawson, *The Making of Europe* (1932 ed.; repr. Washington, DC: The Catholic University of America Press, 2003), pp. 119-20.

these things be?' (John 3:9), 'as if something cannot be unless they understand it'.[59]

Whereas some ascetics—Hieracas crops up again—came to almost dualistic views which claimed that virginity had replaced marriage since the Incarnation, Athanasius proclaimed what he described as 'a single chorus and a single symphony in the faith'.[60] The Lord has saved one church—not a body of ascetics and a body of second-class believers. Indeed, grace could at times sound deceptively simple: 'The Lord has reopened the way for us through his own blood and made it easy.'[61] Nevertheless, the Alexandrian canons prohibited clerics from celebrating the eucharist the same day that they had sexual relations with their wives.[62] Like most clerics of his day, Athanasius had qualms about 'relations of pleasure' in marriage[63]— the Song of Songs was in need of allegorizing.

The Christian was to live simply, and be mindful of the poor, for 'if you are living extravagantly in the feasts of Sodom, fear lest you receive the sufferings of Sodom'.[64] Like John Chrysostom a little later, Athanasius had nothing but scorn for what he called 'hateful slave-trading'.[65] Licentiousness, either in sexuality or in general lifestyle, is fatal to anyone who is seeking to live in Christ. The Christian is to trust Christ and imitate Him, seeking the crown and incorruptible joy: 'For even though, humanly speaking, the labour of such a journey is great, yet the Saviour himself has rendered even it light and kindly.'[66] The feast of the Lord's Supper unites all Christians: 'Since the Saviour is in our midst, we are not far from one another when we celebrate the feast.'[67]

---

59. Brakke, *Athanasius and Asceticism*, p. 61.

60. Ibid., p. 142.

61. Ibid., p. 155.

62. Ibid., p. 185.

63. Ibid., p. 316.

64. Ibid., p. 9315

65. Ibid., p. 318.

66. Athanasius, *Easter Letter* 28 (for 356) (NPNF2 4:550).

67. Brakke, *Athanasius and Asceticism*, p. 162.

The believer had to know Christ first, then follow His laws: 'For when the Guide to the laws is unknown, one does not readily pass on to the observance of them.'[68] He did refer to faith and godliness as sisters,[69] whereas the biblical teaching would consider it better to use the image of 'mother' and 'daughter'– faith leading to godliness. Yet, in 330 the bishop had told his flock that 'faith gives birth to hope and every virtue'.[70] Athanasius always advised the Christian to center his or her thoughts on Christ in order to overcome temptations: 'For you have him in your heart and so you will not stumble in your inner thoughts.'[71] This is because 'where Christ dwells, there is holiness'.[72]

---

68. Athanasius, *Easter Letter* 11.3 (for 339) (NPNF2 4:533).

69. Athanasius, *Easter Letter* 11.9 (for 339) (NPNF2 4:536).

70. Brakke, *Athanasius and Asceticism*, p. 321. This is his *Easter Letter* 24, but Brakke points out that it is actually *Easter Letter 2*.

71. Ibid., p. 287.

72. Ibid., p. 293.

8

'CHRIST LOVED US IN HIS GREAT LOVE AND ASCENDED A CROSS FOR OUR SAKE':

The Influence and Estimation of Athanasius's Life

Estimations of Athanasius

A few years after Athanasius's death, Gregory of Nazianzus delivered an oration in his honor, declaring, 'In praising Athanasius, I shall be praising virtue.'[1] He portrayed him as 'the noble champion of the Word',[2] a man who was 'gentle, free from anger, sympathetic, sweet in words, sweeter in disposition; angelic in appearance, more angelic in mind'.[3] His conduct was even more admirable than his theology.[4] Later, the Abbot Cosmas was to advise that anyone who came across a writing of Athanasius, and had no paper on which to transcribe it, should write it on his clothes.[5] Modern scholars, on the other hand, have fallen over themselves in an attempt to repudiate this view. Yet, Athanasius was the only Christian to attract Edward Gibbon's admiration:

---

1.   Gregory of Nazianzus, *Oration* 21, On the Great Athanasius (NPNF2 7:1).

2.   Ibid., (NPNF2 7:14).

3.   Ibid., (NPNF2 7:9).

4.   Ibid., (NPNF2 7:35).

5.   Cited in F. L. Cross, *The Study of St Athanasius* (Oxford: Clarendon Press, 1945), p. 5.

> Amidst the storms of persecution, the Archbishop of Alexandria
> was patient of labour, jealous of fame, careless of safety; and
> although his mind was tainted by the contagion of fanaticism,
> Athanasius displayed a superiority of character and abilities,
> which would have qualified him, far better than the degenerate
> sons of Constantine, for the government of a great monarchy.[6]

Unlike one of his successors, Cyril, he was never a persecutor; he
was not the 'new Pharaoh'.

After the second Ecumenical Council of Constantinople in
381, Arianism was confined to the barbarian tribes such as the
Vandals and the Visigoths. More than anyone else, Athanasius,
with his resolute character and firmness of faith, was responsible
for that changed situation. Successive emperors wanted Arius
and the Eusebians restored to the church or recognised by her;
but to Athanasius that was out of the question. Hugo Rahner
maintains:

> Arian Christianity was always more prone than the Catholic
> Church to submit to the state's authority because it lacked the
> counterweight of faith in Christ's divinity and thus a sense
> of transcendence, which could lead it to consider the state as
> only a thing of secondary importance compared with Christ's
> supreme power flowing from his participation in the divine
> nature.[7]

G. H. Williams puts forward a not dissimilar interpretation of
events.[8] R. P. C. Hanson mocks this thesis as crude,[9] but it was
Athanasius who first made the angry claim that the Arians had
no king but Caesar. Hanson also ridicules John Henry Newman's

6.   E. Gibbon, *The History of the Decline and Fall of the Roman Empire*, ed. David
      Womersley (Repr. London: Penguin, 1995), ch. 21.

7.   H. Rahner, *Church and State in Early Christianity* (1961 ed.; repr. San Francisco, CA:
      Ignatius Press, 1992), p. 64.

8.   G. H. Williams, 'Christology and Church-State Relations in the Fourth Century,'
      Church History 20, no. 3 (1951): pp. 1-33.

9.   R. P. C. Hanson, *The Search for the Christian Doctrine of God: The Arian Controversy
      318–381* (Edinburgh: T&T Clark, 1988), p. 852.

'romantic suggestion' that it was the common people who held out against heretical emperors.[10] There might be more realism than romanticism to this view in the light of the unwavering support that so many Egyptian Christians gave to Athanasius in his troubles.

At the beginning of the twentieth century, Eduard Schwartz, Otto Seeck and, a little later, H. G. Opitz began the modern trend of dismantling the heroic status of Athanasius and consigning him to what Charles Kannengiesser has called 'a last, and posthumous, century-long exile'.[11] R. P. C. Hanson portrayed him as ruthless and unscrupulous, as one who is 'like an employer of thugs hired to intimidate his enemies'.[12] Hanson does modify this by writing: 'Athanasius, though an unscrupulous politician, was also a genuine theologian.'[13] Frances Young claims, 'He was vehement to the point of violence and his "charity" was the face of an astute politician out to achieve his own ends'.[14]

Timothy Barnes virtually calls him a gangster at the head of 'an ecclesiastical mafia'.[15] He says of Athanasius: 'he could not have cut such an impressive figure had he not been conspicuously lacking in the Christian virtues of meekness and humility'.[16] He adds: 'Athanasius may often disregard or pervert the truth, but he is a subtler and more skilful liar than Schwartz realised.'[17] Richard

---

10. Hanson, *Search for the Christian Doctrine*, p. 851. See John Henry Newman, *On Consulting the Faithful in Matters of Doctrine*, ed. John Coulson (London: Collins, 1986).

11. Cited in David M. Gwynn, *The Eusebians: The Polemic of Athanasius of Alexandria and the Construction of the 'Arian Controversy,'* Oxford Theological Monographs (Oxford: Oxford University Press, 2007), p. 2, n.5. See also Nathan Kwok-kit Ng, *The Spirituality of Athanasius* (Berne: Peter Lang, 2001), pp. 23-24, 24n29.

12. Hanson, *Search for the Christian Doctrine*, p. 254.

13. Ibid., p. 422.

14. Frances Young, *From Nicaea to Chalcedon* (London: SCM, 1983), p. 80.

15. Timothy Barnes, *Constantine and Eusebius* (Cambridge, MA: Harvard University Press, 1981), p. 230.

16. Barnes, *Athanasius and Constantius*, p. 1.

17. Ibid., p. 3.

Rubenstein too says that his ambition was boundless and that he was at home with political skullduggery. With scant regard for historical realities, Athanasius is compared to Luther, Calvin, and Lenin as a master of 'political ruthlessness'.[18] H. Idris Bell considers that there is 'a germ of truth' in the portrayal of Athanasius as self-willed and unruly.[19] Hans von Campenhausen writes of him: 'There was something unGreek about his nature, which is harsh and rigid, without a touch of intellectual grace or charm.'[20] To Robert Payne, 'There was something in him of the temper of the modern dogmatic revolutionary: nothing stopped him.'[21]

C. Wilfred Griggs portrays Athanasius as 'autocratic',[22] and as one who brought all his troubles upon himself:

> One can surmise that if Athanasius had been more like his predecessor, that is to say, more conciliatory and less ruthless and violent toward any who disagreed with him, he might have avoided being exiled so many times and the widening theological gulf of the fourth century might not have occurred.[23]

L. W. Barnard acknowledges the greatness of Athanasius, but adds that 'a spirit of fanaticism clouded his historical judgement leading to unfairness in treating the motives and beliefs of his opponents'.[24] Christopher Haas sees a violent man who has

---

18. Richard Rubenstein, *When Jesus Became God* (New York: Harcourt Brace, 1999), pp. 104-105.

19. H. I. Bell, *Jews and Christians in Egypt* (1924 ed.; repr. Westport, CT: Greenwood Press, 1972), p. 57.

20. Hans von Campenhausen, *The Fathers of the Greek Church* (London: A. & C. Black, 1963), p. 73.

21. Cited in Christopher Hall, 'How Arianism Almost Won,' *Christian History and Biography*, 85 (Winter 2005): p. 38.

22. C. Wilfred Griggs, *Early Egyptian Christianity from its Origins to 451 C.E.* (Leiden: Brill, 1988), p. 137.

23. Ibid., p. 138.

24. Leslie W. Barnard, *Studies in Athanasius' 'Apologia Secunda'* (Bern: Peter Lang, 1992), pp. 7-8.

inflicted on history a 'torrent of self-serving literature'.[25] E. M. Forster asserts: 'He had weaned the Church from her traditions of scholarship and tolerance, the tradition of Clement and Origen'.[26] W. H. C. Frend makes the usual accusation: 'He did not shrink from the use of violence against opponents.' However, says Frend, he mellowed in old age and became 'something of the Grand Old Man of orthodoxy'.[27]

Despite these assertions, it is difficult to view Athanasius as the head of an empire-wide party. Basil of Caesarea and Hilary of Poitiers, for example, seem not to have been greatly influenced by him. Yet a theological convergence took place along with a greater clarity. Certainly Athanasius could be fierce in controversy, but F. L. Cross has reminded us that he was 'a theologian of the market-place rather than the study'.[28] For all his trials and pressures, Athanasius wrote with pity about Liberius of Rome when he fell into error and he was kind to Ossius in his lapse and to those others who signed the creed at Ariminum—a contrast, for example, to the attitude of Lucifer of Cagliari.[29] Having said that, he praised Lucifer, even citing the description of him as 'the Elijah of our times'.[30] He was mild in criticising men like Marcellus and Apollinaris. There is every reason to view him as one who fought for great principles, not for personal power. Sometime after 357 he contended: 'I have suffered these things on account of nothing else but the Arian impiety.'[31]

Athanasius maintained that persecution was of the devil and that 'the truth is not preached with swords or with darts nor by

25. Christopher Haas, *Alexandria in Late Antiquity* (London: The Johns Hopkins University Press, 1997), p. 178.

26. E. M. Forster, *Pharos and Pharillon* (London: The Hogarth Press, 1961), p. 50.

27. W. H. C. Frend, 'Athanasius as an Egyptian Christian Leader in the Fourth Century' in his *Religion Popular and Unpopular in the Early Christian Centuries* (London: Variorum Reprints, 1976), pp. 21, 37.

28. F. L. Cross, *The Study of St Athanasius* (Oxford: Clarendon Press, 1945), p. 5.

29. See Athanasius, *To the Bishops of Egypt* 8.

30. See Athanasius, *Epistles 50-51*.

31. Athanasius, *Defence Against the Arians* 89.

means of soldiers; but by persuasion and counsel'.[32] Indeed, 'it is the part of true godliness not to compel, but to persuade'.[33] In his second *Easter Letter*, dated in 330, he called on his flock to imitate Christ:

> Not only should we bear his image, but should receive from him an example and pattern of heavenly living; that as he has begun, we should go on, that suffering, we should not threaten, being reviled, we should not revile again, but should bless them that curse, and in everything commit ourselves to God who judges righteously.[34]

It was the lot of the Christian to suffer, not to persecute: 'those who suffer temporal afflictions here, finally having endured, attain comfort, while those who here persecute are trodden under foot, and have no good end'.[35]

In Athanasius, pastoral concern took precedence over polemics, as can be seen by the general tone of his Easter Letters. His very first *Easter Letter*, for the year 329, reveals his warm-hearted spirit:

> Let us remember the poor, and not forget kindness to strangers; above all, let us love God with all our soul, and might, and strength, and our neighbour as ourselves. So may we receive those things which the eye has not seen, nor the ear heard, and which have not entered into the heart of man, which God has prepared for those who love him, through his only Son, our Lord and Saviour, Jesus Christ; through whom, to the Father alone, by the Holy Spirit, be glory and dominion for ever and ever. Amen.[36]

---

32. Athanasius, *History of the Arians* 33.

33. Ibid., 67.

34. Athanasius, *Easter Letter* 2.5, slightly altered.

35. Ibid., 10.6 (for 338).

36. Ibid., 1.11, slightly altered.

His writings could be polemical, but he never lost sight of the goal of the Christian Faith: to love and glorify God and to grow in His grace.

These were troubled times—most times are—and history-writing thrives on troubles. Socrates commented: 'I myself should have been silent, if the Church had remained undisturbed by divisions.'[37] In the midst of the turmoil, Athanasius bore a faithful testimony. As G. L. Prestige notes: 'Single-hearted and sometimes almost single-handed, he had saved the Church from capture by pagan intellectualism ... By his tenacity and vision in preaching one God and one Saviour, he had preserved from dissolution the unity and integrity of the Christian faith.'[38] John Behr also states: 'Nicene Christianity exists by virtue of his constancy and vision.'[39] C. S. Lewis agreed: 'It is his glory that he did not move with the times; it is his reward that he now remains when those times, as all times do, have moved away.'[40] Which is why, in both his life and his teaching, Athanasius is worthy of study today.

Not all that Athanasius said on the atonement can be regarded as adequate and not all of his views on monastic asceticism can be endorsed, but his achievements are worthy of appreciation. Theologically, he testified to the full deity of the Son and later to the full deity of the Spirit. Spiritually, he waged a lifelong war at considerable personal cost to himself to maintain his testimony to the biblical revelation that God is triune and did so while maintaining his own humble walk with God. Pastorally, he preserved the unity and witness of most of the Alexandrian churches to this truth in most unpromising

---

37. Socrates, *Church History* 1.18.

38. G. L. Prestige, *Fathers and Heretics* (repr. 1968; London: SPCK, 1940), p. 76.

39. John Behr, *Formation of Christian Theology: The Nicene Faith, volume 2, part 1* (Crestwood, NY: St Vladimir's Seminary Press, 2004), p. 167.

40. C. S. Lewis, 'Introduction to Athanasius' in *Athanasius: On the Incarnation*, Popular Patristics Series 44B (Repr. Crestwood, NY: St Vladimir's Seminary Press, 2011), pp. 8–9.

circumstances. Athanasius was a man remembered as one who lived *contra mundum*, but only because he lived first and foremost as a servant of and witness to the Word made flesh, Jesus Christ.

Sozomen wrote of 'the esteem in which Athanasius was universally held'[41]—a view which ought not to be lightly dismissed as short-sighted hagiography. In Athanasius there was an admirable combination of theological clarity and firmness of resolve, a commitment to truth without blinkered fanaticism, an asceticism which yet remained in the world, and a pastoral heart without any tendency to sentimentality. Athanasius's own words make a fitting conclusion and appeal:

> Christ loved us in his great love and ascended a cross for our sake ... His disciples believed that it was truly he who rose from the dead. Immediately they knelt down and worshipped him and knew without a doubt that he is the true God ... Let us too, beloved brothers, kneel with a true heart and worship him truly and his holy cross, for he is the Lord of all. And whoever believes in him truly will not be put to shame.[42]

Athanasius was indeed prepared to be a man *against the world* because he was a man *in* Christ and *for* Christ.

---

41. Sozomen, *Church History* VI.12.

42. Cited in David Brakke, *Athanasius and Asceticism* (London: John Hopkins University Press, 1998), p. 318.

BRIEF GLOSSARY

Third-century theologies

Monarchianism or Sabellianism: the belief that there is only one Person in the Godhead, who appears in various modes or roles.

Novatianism: a view held by a purist group that appeared in the 250s during the persecution and that argued that the Great Church was apostate. They were Trinitarian in their beliefs.

Fourth-century theologies

Anomoeans or Anomoians or Eunomians: those who believed that the Son is unlike the Father in essence.

Apollinarianism: the belief taught by Apollinaris that the divine Word took the place of the soul in Jesus Christ. This would mean that the Word possessed only a human body, not a human soul.

Arianism: derived from the teaching of Arius, who contended that Christ is the highest of the angels, not the eternal and divine Son of God.

Donatists: a purist group which split from the church at Carthage in North Africa, claiming that the Catholic Church was apostate and only the Donatist Church provided salvation.

Macedonians (also known at Tropici or Pneumatomachi): groups of professing Christians who did not believe in the deity of the Holy Spirit.

Key figures

Eusebius of Caesarea: known as a church historian, but as a theologian he was more sympathetic to Arius than to Athanasius.

Eusebius of Nicomedia: not to be confused with his namesake from Caesarea. He was decidedly pro-Arian.

Marcellus of Ancyra: an ally of Athanasius in some ways, but suspected of holding views that were tainted with Sabellianism.

Melitius of Lycopolis: an Egyptian bishop who was sent to the mines around 305–306 and came to oppose Peter, the bishop of Alexandria, at the time. Melitius was probably a rigorist who thought Peter was too lax in allowing Christians who lapsed during the persecution to return to communion with the church.

Theological terms

Homoiousios: a Greek word meaning 'like essence', used to describe the belief that the Son is like the Father in essence. Athanasius came to realise that some of these believed in the full deity of the Son in that He is like the Father in every way.

Homoousios: a term used in the Nicene creed to describe the Son as of the same essence as the Father.

Hypostasis: a somewhat flexible word which in the West was often used to mean 'essence' (*ousia*), but in the East often meant 'person' (*prosōpon*).

Also available from Christian Focus ...

EARLY CHURCH FATHERS
SERIES EDITOR MICHAEL A. G. HAYKIN

PATRICK

OF HIS LIFE
& IMPACT

IRELAND

MICHAEL A. G. HAYKIN

Patrick of Ireland
His Life and Impact
Michael A. G. Haykin

Patrick ministered to kings and slaves alike in the culture
that had enslaved him. Patrick's faith and his commitment
to the Word of God through hard times is a true example of
the way that God calls us to grow and to bless those around
us through our suffering. Michael Haykin's masterful
biography of Patrick's life and faith will show you how you
can follow God's call in your life.

Early Church Fathers: this series relates the magnificent
impact that those fathers of the early church made for our
world today.

ISBN: 978-1-5271-0100-5

EARLY CHURCH FATHERS
SERIES EDITOR MICHAEL A. G. HAYKIN

CYPRIAN
OF
HIS LIFE
& IMPACT
CARTH-
AGE

BRIAN ARNOLD

Cyprian of Carthage
His Life and Impact
Brian J. Arnold

Cyprian of Carthage's story is one of incredible perseverance for the sake of the gospel. Living through a time of terrible persecution towards Christians, Cyprian wrestled with questions surrounding the church and contributed greatly to the writings on its importance as the bride of Christ. He dealt first-hand with the effects which persecution has on church bodies and offered many insights which are becoming increasingly relevant in the West today.

ISBN: 978-1-5271-0099-2

CHRISTIAN
HERITAGE

Daily Readings

The
Early
Church
Fathers

Edited by
Nick
Needham

Daily Readings
The Early Church Fathers
Nick Needham

- Daily reading gift book
- Beautifully bound and presented
- Wisdom from the first interpreters of Scripture

The early church fathers have always had a special place in Christian theology. As the first interpreters of the gospel, we often find in their words a sense of the gospel's sheer freshness and reality. More than this, they were the thinkers who first hammered out the full meaning of what Scripture says about the Trinity and the person of Christ. Their sayings, presented here by Nick Needham, are more than just relevant - they present the opportunity to kindle within us something of that same healthy and godly spirit.

ISBN: 978-1-5271-0043-5

Christian Focus Publications

Our mission statement –

STAYING FAITHFUL

In dependence upon God we seek to impact the world through literature faithful to His infallible Word, the Bible. Our aim is to ensure that the Lord Jesus Christ is presented as the only hope to obtain forgiveness of sin, live a useful life and look forward to heaven with Him.

Our Books are published in four imprints:

CHRISTIAN FOCUS

popular works including biographies, commentaries, basic doctrine and Christian living.

CHRISTIAN HERITAGE

books representing some of the best material from the rich heritage of the church.

MENTOR

books written at a level suitable for Bible College and seminary students, pastors, and other serious readers. The imprint includes commentaries, doctrinal studies, examination of current issues and church history.

CF4•K

children's books for quality Bible teaching and for all age groups: Sunday school curriculum, puzzle and activity books; personal and family devotional titles, biographies and inspirational stories – Because you are never too young to know Jesus!

Christian Focus Publications Ltd,
Geanies House, Fearn, Ross-shire,
IV20 1TW, Scotland, United Kingdom.
www.christianfocus.com